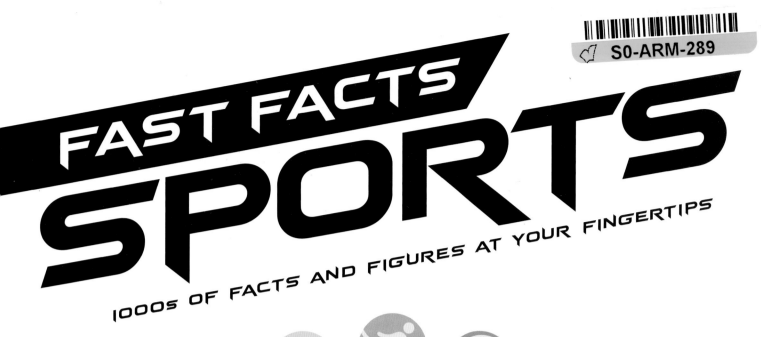

FAST FACTS
SPORTS

1000s OF FACTS AND FIGURES AT YOUR FINGERTIPS

Kane Miller
A DIVISION OF EDC PUBLISHING

First American Edition 2019
Kane Miller, A Division of EDC Publishing

Copyright © Green Android Ltd 2018

For information contact:
Kane Miller, A Division of EDC Publishing
P.O. Box 470663
Tulsa, OK 74147-0663
www.kanemiller.com
www.edcpub.com
www.usbornebooksandmore.com

ISBN: 978-1-61067-832-2
Library of Congress Control Number: 2018942393

Written and edited by Lyn Coutts
Stadium illustrations courtesy of Peter Bull Art Studio

Printed in China, May 2019.

Image Credits:
Images © shutterstock.com: france celebrates after winning the fifa 2018 © a.ricardo, bengals and colts line-up © alexey stiop, usain bolt (on cover) © cp dc press, marianne vos © jan de wild, serena williams (on cover), michael phelps © leonard zhukovsky, roger federer © lev radin, cristiano ronaldo (on cover), cristiano ronaldo © marco iacobucci ep, michael phelps (on cover), hermann maier, brian o'driscoll © mitch gunn, irish fans cheering at rugby world cup © paolo bona, simone biles (on cover) © petr toman, mat hoffman © tinseltown.

Images © dreamstime.com: bobby orr, earvin magic johnson, joe montana, michael jordan, tom brady, jack nicklaus, jerry rice, tom brady © jerry coli, serena williams © ocusfocus, lin dan © pariyawit, sukumpantanasarn, michael schumacher © sandrarbarba, shaun white, rafael nadal © zhukovsky. image © wikicommons: bjorn dunderbeck © andy khitrovo, jackie joyner-kersee © ash carter, dara torres © bryan Allison, michael phelps © bryan allison, gregor schlierenzauer © christian bier, brad bowden © connormah, georgeta damian © cortix93, barry lamar bonds © creative commons attribution, desafio de campeões © editorial j, pele © el gráfico #2624, usain bolt © erik van leeuwen, marit bjørgen © frankie fouganthin, alain prost © gahetna in het nationnal archief, lauren 'loz' jackson © gina, wayne gretzky © hakandahlstrom, ben ainslie © hpeterswald, oksana masters © irongargoyle, jason kenny © jim thurston, jan-ove waldener © kanjitard, mike trout © keith allison on flickr, triscia zorn © laurahale, babe ruth © library of congress's prints and photographs division, rocky marciano © mohamed said momo, siamand rahman © mohammad delkesh, isabell werth © oliver abels, jessica fox © ollie harding from london, uk, frankie dettori © paul friel from guildford, uk – flickr, sugar ray robinson © juan manuel fangio, gordie howe, nadia comăneci, george eyser, mark spitz, dezső gyarmati, oliver halassy, elisabeta lipă, gert fredriksson, sydney barnes, reiner klimke, hubert van innis © public domain, lindsay vonn © stefan brending, tiger woods © tim hipps, tony mccoy © www.pbase.com/amoore/the_cheltenham_festival_2006, lionel messi ©.

Images © getty images: jahanghir khan © bob thomas / contributor, steve redgrave © clive brunskill/allsport, yasuhiro yamashita © david finch / contributor, sarah ayton © david rogers / staff, babe didrikson zaharias © hulton archive / stringer, patrick anderson © jamie mcdonald / staff, karch kiraly © jeff gross / staff, ragnhild myklebust © john g. mabanglo / stringer john g, fedor the last emperor © josh hedges/forza llc / contributor, guo wenjun © lars baron / staff, esther vergeer © leon neal/ staffleon neal / staff, hadi saei © quinn rooney, dmitri sautin © quinn rooney/getty images, kimberly rhode © sam greenwood / staff, muhammad ali © the stanley weston archive, greg louganis © tony duffy/allsport, arnold palmer © transcendental graphics.

Images © alamy.com: anastasia davydova © aflo co., ltd, carl osburn © historic collection.

Other images: koehi uchimura © www.edubilla.com, guo jingjing © flickr.com fotoseletras, emma booth © julie Wilson, darrell pace © crawford family u.s. olympic archives, united states olympic, pyross dimas © althistory.wikia.com/wiki/civciv5, leeanne Hewitt © damon higgins/the palm beach post, ibrahim hamadto © ittf meetings, lindy hou © www.lindyhou.com.

▼ CONTENTS

→ Introduction	4
⊕ Fast Facts up close	5
SOCCER	6
FOOTBALL	10
ATHLETICS	14
BASEBALL	18
BASKETBALL	22
BOXING	24
COMBAT SPORTS	25
MOTORSPORTS	26
TENNIS	30

 **OTHER RACQUET SPORTS** 32

 **GOLF** 34

 ICE HOCKEY 36

 GYMNASTICS 38

 SWIMMING 40

 DIVING 42

 OTHER POOL SPORTS 43

 ROWING 44

 CANOEING 46

 SAILING 47

ALPINE SKIING 48

 OTHER WINTER SPORTS 50

 RUGBY 52

 CRICKET 53

 HORSE RACING 54

 EQUESTRIAN SPORTS 55

 ARCHERY 56

 SHOOTING 57

 CYCLING 58

 VOLLEYBALL 62

 OLYMPIC WEIGHTLIFTING 63

 Country codes
 Sports governing bodies 64

Introduction

Can you imagine our planet without sports? No races, no football games, no swim meets; no fields, no courts, no athletics tracks – and no trophies, medals, glorious victories or crushing defeats. It's almost unimaginable if you're a sports fan, an active participant, or spectator. Games and sports have been part of the global human story for several thousand years. Games have always had cultural, political and religious significance. The ancient Romans used sports to rally citizens, so chariot racers had team names, and victorious gladiators were hailed as heroes. Their records of wins and losses were possibly sports' first set of stats!

> "The reason sport is attractive to many is that it's filled with reversals. What you think may happen doesn't happen. A champion is beaten, an unknown becomes a champion."
> Roger Bannister (1929–2018), British athlete

Sports at its best

Skill
One of baseball's greatest moments, in 1951, Bobby Thomson hit a home run – the "shot heard round the world" – to capture a 5-4 win and the NL pennant for the New York Giants over the Brooklyn Dodgers.

Sporting spirit
With the end of the Triathlon World Series (Mexico 2016) within sight, Alistair Brownlee helped his exhausted brother, Jonathan, reach the finish, showing spirit, loyalty and love – and sacrificing his chance of winning.

Athleticism
Cristiano Ronaldo's bicycle kick – his right foot arcing 9 feet above the ground – secured his second Real Madrid goal against Juventus in the April 2018 Champions League. Was this Ronaldo's greatest-ever goal? Who knows?

Sports hall of shame

Match fixing
Known as the Black Sox scandal, eight members of the Chicago White Sox baseball team were charged with throwing the 1919 World Series in exchange for money from a gambling syndicate. All were banned from pro baseball.

Unfair play
Diego Maradona's goal in the 51st minute of the 1986 FIFA World Cup quarterfinal – Argentina v. England – was scored with his hand. Maradona himself dubbed it the "Hand of God" goal, but everyone else called it cheating.

Win at all costs
In March 2018, Australian cricketer Cameron Bancroft was televised roughing up the ball with sandpaper in the Third Test against South Africa. Three Australian players were banned for their roles in this ball-tampering incident.

What is a Sport?

A sport is any activity that has rules, a competitive element, and requires skill, mental application, physical prowess, stamina and dexterity. A sport is open to enthusiastic novices, dedicated amateurs and paid professionals. At its simplest it can be one person running to record a personal best. At its most complicated 32 NFL teams, each with a 53-player roster, play 256 games over a 17-week season according to a rule book that runs to 70,000 words!

Sports ancient...
Among the oldest sports are wrestling – its first rule book was written on papyrus 2,200 years ago – and tsu' chu – a Chinese game of football dating from 2500 BCE. Other early sports were running (the only event in the first Olympics in 776 BCE), archery, gymnastics, horse and chariot racing, boxing, javelin and discus. Many heroes of ancient battles first proved themselves in sports.

On July 15, 2018, the French soccer team raised the trophy as FIFA World Cup champions after they defeated Croatia 4–2.

On your marks...
More than being great for personal fitness, sports are fun, sociable, and foster team spirit, confidence and fair play. Sports ignites passion among athletes, fans, and even couch potatoes! *Fast Facts* will make you not just a player or a fan, but an expert on the world's most popular sports. At your fingertips are the history, rules, teams, stars, records and stats. On your marks, get set, go *Fast Facts*! Sports rule!

...and modern
The big difference between ancient and modern sports is numbers. There are now about 8,000 types of sports played worldwide, with billions of participants and spectators, thousands of official sports organizations, hundreds of huge global tournaments and events, and 24/7 coverage. Increased funding means that highly trained and supported elite sportspeople are relegating yesterday's records to history.

Irish fans celebrate their team's 32-17 game win over Namibia in the 2007 Rugby World Cup. (Neither team made it past the group stage.)

The Cincinnati Bengals and the Indianapolis Colts line up during a regular season game. The Colts won 13–10 after a closing seconds touchdown.

Fast Facts up close

Each section starts with an overview of aims and rules, along with background information and a quote. Sports are not just action packed – it's a numbers game. Some charts and features give the critical times, speeds, heights, scores and medal tallies. Others cover heart thumping and heartbreaking moments and the arenas that hosted them. Charts and features are identified by an icon.

Record Breakers

These top times, speeds, distances, scores and more are extracted from the archives of the sport's governing body and other official records*.

* All records and statistics are current to July 2018.

A Moment in Time

This feature highlights the "Wow" moments – the unforgettable and astonishing things that changed a predicted outcome or even the sport itself!

Controversy

Whenever there is competition and the pursuit of glory, there is controversy. This feature looks at close finishes, skullduggery and shameful behavior.

Focus on the Olympics

Summer Winter

Showcasing individual, team, and country records for the Games, this section also includes profiles of outstanding Olympians.

Para Athletes

The spotlight is on a para sport, its international and Paralympic records, its record makers and breakers, and its superstars.

Sporting Arenas

Fast Facts introduces the stadiums – ancient, iconic and cutting-edge – where magic and controversial moments play out for all to witness.

Super Teams

Featuring the football, soccer, basketball and baseball teams who clinched victory from defeat, won every trophy or had a lineup of stars to take your breath away.

★★★★★★★★★★

Super team rating
Do you agree with *Fast Facts'* star rating out of 10?

Team colors
Use these color representations to spot your team.

All-Stars

There are sporting heroes aplenty, but *Fast Facts* has chosen just three legends of yesterday and today in each sport – some you'll know, others you might not.

Maps

Colorful and clearly labeled, these pinpoint the home cities of teams and the locations of some major events and tournaments.

Superstar

This section focuses on a sportsperson mentioned in a relevant list, filling out their profile with other achievements or background information.

Sports governing bodies

Each sport has a national or international organization to coordinate major events and set regulations. *See page 64.*

Epic Encounter

A special head-to-head moment, often a grudge match, local derby or longtime rivalry, between two teams, countries or athletes is profiled.

Player Profile

Highlighting an athlete or player and their contribution to a match or event, these profiles are not always about winners, but also share the lessons of losing.

Team Profile

The scores, events and people that made a team great: discover the teams that came to dominate a sport, sometimes for decades.

Trophies and Awards

Learn about the trophies, cups, belts and bowls that await the glorious victors. Many are solid gold, but their true value to a sportsperson is priceless.

Current Champions

Examine the individual, team or country that currently holds a sport's highest honor, and their route to the record books.

Runners-up

It's not just about the winners and losers – for some teams or athletes, it's always the silver and never the gold or the dizzy height of the podium's top step.

FIFA

What do these icons mean?

To save space (so more *Fast Facts* could be included), icons replace headings in the charts and features. Use this list to become familiar with what each icon represents, and refer back to this page as you need. There's a lot to take in!

Player/athlete name

Player/athlete age

Country
Where necessary, IOC or FIFA three-letter codes are used instead of country names. *See page 64.*

Player/athlete appearances

Player/athlete career years

Weight category
The weight class in which a weight- or powerlifter competes.

Club/team name

Key players

Epic encounter

Date of event

Year last won

Olympic year

Soccer: goals scored

Football: points scored

Football: Super Bowl appearance

Football: number of touchdowns scored

Basketball: points scored

Golf hole

Golf score

Rugby score

Cycling: overall winner

Horse name

Races run by a horse

Money won/earned

Record

Total

Record time
This is shown as hours: minutes: seconds. hundredths of a second (0:0:00.000).

Distance, length or height in meters (m) or kilometers (km), except for the mile race and some US-based motorsports (expressed in miles/mi.).

Speed in kph or kph/mph

Number of titles/wins

Gold medal/s

Silver medal/s

Bronze medal/s

Total medal tally

Runner-up

Podium finish

Event

Location

Arena capacity

Year built

Michael Phelps breaking his world record and winning gold in the 200-meter butterfly final in the 2009 World Championships in Italy.

SOCCER

Known as football throughout much of the world, this contact sport is played by over 250 million worldwide, and its World Cup attracts up to 3.2 billion viewers. The Football Association (FA) established the rules of the game in 1863, but "kick ball" started in China in 220 BCE. Two teams of 11 aim to score goals in the opposition's net. The goalkeeper can use hands and arms on the round ball within his or her own penalty area. All other players kick or head the ball, except in a throw-in. A game consists of two halves of 45 minutes. In knockout competitions, a tied game is followed by two 15-minute periods, and then, if the score remains tied, a penalty shoot-out.

> "Some people believe football is a matter of life and death... I can assure you it is much, much more important than that."
>
> Bill Shankly (1913–1981), Scottish soccer player and manager

All-Stars

Pelé

🔄 1953–1977   🏳 Brazil

Pelé (a nickname he chose) was 11 when he was first picked for a team. Just six years later he became the youngest player to score in a World Cup match. This Brazilian forward went on to play 1,363 games and score 1,281 goals.

Cristiano Ronaldo

🔄 1992–   🏳 Portugal

This Portuguese forward is regarded as the best player of all time, and his five Ballon d'Or awards back this up. He tops the goals-scored records, and hat tricks come regularly. Ronaldo moved in 2018 from Real Madrid to Juventus.

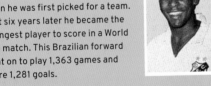

Lionel Messi

🔄 1994–   🏳 Argentina

Messi's record rivals that of Ronaldo – five Ballon d'Ors and there is only a small difference in goals and hat tricks scored. This Argentinian legend has played forward for Barcelona his whole professional career.

Record Breakers

Highest scorers of MLS*

👤	🔄	⚽
Landon Donovan	2001–2016	145
Chris Wondolowski	2005–	134
Jeff Cunningham	1998–2010	134
Jaime Moreno	1996–2010	133
Ante Razov	1996–2009	114

* MLS (Major League Soccer): this is the highest level of professional soccer in Canada and the US.

Highest scorers of EPL*

👤	🔄	⚽
Alan Shearer	1992–2006	260
Wayne Rooney	2001–2018	208
Andrew Cole	1993–2008	187
Frank Lampard	1993–2015	177
Thierry Henry	1999–2012	175

* EPL (English Premier League): this began as the Football Association (FA) Premier League and it is the top level of professional soccer in England.

Highest scorers of Ligue 1*

👤	🔄	⚽
Delio Onnis	1971–1986	299
Bernard Lacombe	1969–1987	255
Hervé Revelli	1965–1978	216
Roger Courtois	1932–1956	210
Thadée Cisowski	1947–1961	206

* Ligue 1 (League 1): this is the top level of professional soccer in France. Season winners receive l'Hexagoal trophy.

Most Ballon d'Or* wins

👤	🏳	🏆
Lionel Messi	ARG	5
Cristiano Ronaldo	POR	5
Michel Platini	FRA	3
Johan Cruyff	NED	3
Marco van Basten	NED	3
Franz Beckenbauer	GER	2
Ronaldo	BRA	2
Alfredo Di Stéfano	ESP	2
Kevin Keegan	ENG	2
Karl-Heinz Rummenigge	GER	2

* Ballon d'Or (Golden Ball): this is awarded to the best player of the year as voted by French sports journalists. This list covers winners to December 2017.

Highest transfer fees

👤	🛡	💰
Neymar	Paris Saint-Germain	$289
Philippe Coutinho	Barcelona	$137
Cristiano Ronaldo	Juventus	$137
Ousmane Dembele	Barcelona	$126
Paul Pogba	Manchester United	$116
Gareth Bale	Real Madrid	$112

💰 Value in millions of US dollars. Current to July 2018.

Highest scorers of La Liga*

👤	🔄	⚽
Lionel Messi	2004–	383
Cristiano Ronaldo	2009–2018	311
Telmo Zarra	1940–1955	251
Hugo Sánchez	1981–1994	234
Raúl	1994–2010	228

* La Liga (The League): this is the premier level of professional soccer in Spain.

Highest scorers of the Bundesliga*

👤	🔄	⚽
Gerd Müller	1963–1979	365
Klaus Fischer	1966–1988	268
Jupp Heynckes	1964–1978	220
Manfred Burgsmüller	1967–1990	213
Claudio Pizarro	1999–2017	192

* Bundesliga (Federal League): this is the top level of professional soccer in Germany. Season winners are awarded the Meisterschale.

Highest scorers of Serie A*

👤	🔄	⚽
Silvio Piola	1929–1954	274
Francesco Totti	1992–2017	250
Gunnar Nordahl	1948–1958	225
Giuseppe Meazza	1929–1947	216
José Altafini	1958–1976	216

* Serie A: this is the top level of professional soccer in Italy. Season winners are awarded the Coppa Campioni d'Italia.

Most African Player of the Year* wins

👤	🏳	🏆
Yaya Touré	CIV	4
Samuel Eto'o	CMR	4
George Weah	LBR	3
Abedi Pele	GHA	3
Didier Drogba	CIV	2
El Hadji Diouf	SEN	2
Nwankwo Kanu	NGR	2
Roger Milla	CMR	2
Thomas N'Kono	CMR	2

* African Player of the Year: awarded 1970–1994 by France Football and from 1992 onward by the Confederation of African Football to the best African player in any league each year.

Richest clubs in world football

🏅	🏳	💰
Manchester United	ENG	$756
Real Madrid	ESP	$753
Barcelona	ESP	$725
Bayern Munich	GER	$658
Manchester City	ENG	$591
Paris St-Germain	FRA	$507
Arsenal	ENG	$456

💰 Value in millions of US dollars. Current to April 2018. Ten of the top 20 rich clubs are EPL.

Champions League/European Cup UEFA

Games between European clubs hark back to the 1890s, but the first European Cup kicked off in 1955. This cup became the Champions League in 1992. Over the decades there have been tragedies, like the death of Juventus fans in 1985 at Heysel Stadium, Belgium, and triumphs, like the magic of players such as Eusébio, Johan Cruyff, Franz Beckenbauer and Barcelona's "Dream Team."

Champions League/European Cup club winners*

🛡	▐	📅 ★	🏆	②
Real Madrid	ESP	2018	13	3
Milan	ITA	2007	7	4
Bayern Munich	GER	2013	5	5
Barcelona	ESP	2015	5	3
Liverpool	ENG	2005	5	3
Ajax	NED	1995	4	2
Internazionale	ITA	2010	3	2
Manchester United	ENG	2008	3	2
Juventus	ITA	1996	2	7
Benfica	POR	1962	2	5
Nottingham Forest	ENG	1980	2	0
Porto	POR	2004	2	0

* **Winners:** this list represents the top 12 clubs from the 35 European city clubs that have competed 1955–May 2018.

Top three nations, by wins in finals

▐	🏆	②
Spain	18	11
Italy	12	16
England	12	8

Top Champions League* scorers

👤	▐	🛡	⚽
Cristiano Ronaldo	POR	Manchester United Real Madrid	120
Lionel Messi	ARG	Barcelona	100
Raúl González	ESP	Real Madrid Schalke 04	71
Ruud van Nistelrooy	NED	PSV Eindhoven Manchester United Real Madrid	56
Karim Benzema	FRA	Lyon Real Madrid	56

Most Champions League appearances*

👤	▐	🛡	✅
Iker Casillas	ESP	Real Madrid Porto	167
Cristiano Ronaldo	POR	Manchester United Real Madrid	153
Xavi Hernández	ESP	Barcelona	151
Raúl González	ESP	Real Madrid Schalke 04	142
Ryan Giggs	ENG	Manchester United	141

* Scorers and appearances 1955–May 2018.

Factfile

Mohamed "Mo" Salah

Salah started playing in the Egyptian (his home nation) Premier League, then moved to Europe. He signed to Liverpool in 2017 for a club-record fee. This forward has won many awards, including a Golden Boot (32 goals in 36 league games) and Player of the Year (2018).

2005 "Miracle of Istanbul"
Milan v. Liverpool

With 10 Champions League titles between them, Milan entered Istanbul's Atatürk Stadium as the favorite. At half time, Milan led 3–0. Liverpool tied with three goals in six minutes and went on to win the penalty shoot-out 3–2, in the game known as the "Miracle of Istanbul."

Copa Libertadores de América CONMEBOL

Founded in 1960, this is the premier tournament (named in honor of those who liberated the continent from Spanish and Portuguese rule) in South and Central America. It is contested by 38 clubs and runs from February to December, when the finals are played. The winning club is awarded a trophy simply known as "La Copa." Though a transcontinental competition, it attracts millions of viewers around the world.

Most wins in Copa Libertadores finals*

🛡	▐	📅 ★	🏆	②
Independiente	ARG	1984	7	0
Boca Juniors	ARG	2007	6	4
Peñarol	URU	1987	5	5
Estudiantes	ARG	2009	4	1
Olimpia	PAR	2002	3	4
São Paulo	BRA	2005	3	3
Nacional	URU	1988	3	3
River Plate	ARG	2015	3	2
Grêmio	BRA	2017	3	2
Santos	BRA	2011	3	1
Cruzeiro	BRA	1997	2	2
Internacional	BRA	2010	2	1
Atlético Nacional	COL	2016	2	1

* All lists current to November 2017 end of season finals.

Top three nations, by wins in finals

▐	🏆	②
Argentina	24	10
Brazil	18	15
Uruguay	8	8

Top Copa Libertadores scorers

👤	▐	🛡	⚽
Alberto Spencer	ECU	Peñarol Barcelona	54
Fernando Morena	URU	Peñarol	37
Pedro Rocha	URU	Peñarol São Paulo Palmeiras	36
Daniel Onega*	ARG	River Plate	31
Julio Morales	URU	Nacional	30

* Onega's 31 goals were scored in only 47 games. His goal ratio was 0.66.

Most Copa Libertadores appearances

👤	▐	🛡	✅
Ever Hugo Almeida	PAR	Olimpia	113
Antony de Ávila	COL	América Barcelona	94
Vladimir Soria	BOL	Bolívar	93
Willington Ortiz	COL	Millonarios América Deportivo Cali	92
Rogério Ceni	BRA	São Paulo	90

Factfile

Alberto Spencer

Known as "Cabeza Mágica" (Magic Head), Spencer is hailed a hero in Ecuador and Uruguay. He was capped by both countries. This forward could kick goals with both feet – his La Copa goal record still stands – and his pace let him slice through and past defenses.

Club Atlético Independiente

Based in Avellaneda, Argentina, this club once won a match with only eight men on the field! In international tournaments, it holds 19 titles. Four of its seven La Copa wins were in a row (1972–1975). Arsenio Erico tops the Argentine list of top scorers (295).

World Cup

FIFA

The first World Cup was in 1930, and it is held every four years. In the two years before each tournament, qualifying games between 211 senior men's national squads will determine the 32 (this could increase to 48) teams that will compete in the month-long event. The World Cup attracts more viewers than the Olympics! In 2006, it was estimated that a ninth of the world's population watched the finals.

World Cup winners and runners-up

🏳	🏆	🥈	📅
Brazil	5	2	1958, 1962, 1970, 1994, 2002
Germany	4	4	1954, 1974, 1990, 2014
Italy	4	2	1934, 1938, 1982, 2006
Argentina	2	3	1978, 1986
France	2	1	1998, 2018
Uruguay	2	0	1930, 1950
England	1	0	1966
Spain	1	0	2010
Netherlands	0	3	
Czechoslovakia TCH	0	2	
Hungary	0	2	
Sweden	0	1	
Croatia	0	1	

Players with most tournament participations

👤	🏳	✅	⚽
Rafael Marquez	MEX	5	3
Antonio Carbajal	MEX	5	0
Lothar Matthäus	GER	5	6
Gianluigi Buffon	ITA	5	0

All-time player appearances, by matches

👤	🏳	✅	⚽
Lothar Matthäus	GER	25	6
Miroslav Klose	GER	24	16
Paolo Maldini	ITA	23	0
Diego Maradona	ARG	21	8
Uwe Seeler	GER	21	9
Władysław Żmuda	POL	21	0

Top goal scorers

👤	🏳	⚽	✅
Miroslav Klose	GER	16	24
Ronaldo	BRA	15	19
Gerd Müller	GER	14	13
Just Fontaine	FRA	13	6
Pelé	BRA	12	14
Jürgen Klinsmann	GER	11	17
Sándor Kocsis	HUN	11	5

The most goals scored at a World Cup is 171 (1998, 2014). In 2018 there were 169 back-of-the-net moments.

Factfile

 World Cup Trophy

The original trophy, named for then FIFA president Jules Rimet, was retained by Brazil for its three cup wins, then later stolen and never found. The current 18K gold trophy has two figures holding up the globe.

"The day football died"
Brazil v. Italy

Brazil's record and attacking style was tipped to beat Italy's defensive game in the group stage final of the 1982 World Cup. But Italy's organized play and Paolo Rossi's hat trick won the day. This match saw the rise of this method and the fall of the vibrant free-flowing game.

Women's World Cup

FIFA

The women's World Cup operates in a similar fashion to the men's, but only 24 teams can make it to the final tournament. The first World Cup event was held in 1991, but women's matches attracted large crowds during World War I. This "golden age" ended when the Football Association banned women's football. The ban was not lifted until 1971!

Winners and runners-up

🏳	🏆	🥈	📅★
USA	3	1	2015
Germany	2	1	2007
Japan	1	1	2011
Norway	1	1	1995
Brazil	0	1	
Sweden	0	1	
China	0	1	

Top goal scorers

👤	🏳	⚽
Marta	BRA	15
Birgit Prinz	GER	14
Abby Wambach	USA	14
Michelle Akers	USA	12
Sun Wen	CHN	11
Bettina Wiegmann	GER	11
Ann Kristin Aarønes	NOR	10
Heidi Mohr	GER	10

Factfile

Marta Vieira da Silva

This Brazilian player scored a record 15 goals in World Cups. A star forward, she has been World Player of the Year five times. She currently plays for the Orlando Pride, in Florida.

Team USA

This is soccer's most successful women's team. Its 1999 World Cup final against China is legend. With 0–0 after extra time and 4–4 in the penalty shoot-out, Team USA left back Brandi Chastain scored.

Focus on the Olympics

The men's soccer program has been in the Olympics since the beginning, and women's soccer was added in 1996. Until the 1984 games, it was a purely amateur event. Now, so that the Olympics, with its professional players, does not compete with the World Cup, Olympic squads consist of under-23s with just three over-23s.

Multiple gold-winning nations

🏳	●	●	●	○
Men				
Hungary	3	1	1	5
United Kingdom	3	0	0	3
Argentina	2	2	0	4
Soviet Union URS	2	0	3	5
Uruguay	2	0	0	2
Women				
USA	4	1	0	5

Top goal scorers

👤	🏳	⚽
Men		
Sophus Nielsen*	DEN	14
Antai Dunai	HUN	13
Women		
Cristiane	BRA	14

* In the 2008 Olympics, Nielsen scored a record 10 goals in one game.

Factfile

Cristiane Rozeira de Souza Silva

Known simply as Cristiane, this Brazilian forward has played in four Olympics, won two silvers, and was top goal scorer in 2004. She scored two hat tricks, including the fastest in Olympic records.

 Brazil under-23s

Brazil men's team had three Olympic silver and two bronze, but gold eluded them until 2016 under Neymar's captaincy. The women's squad, with two silvers, still waits for gold.

Super Teams

Brazil national team
 1970

Under a searing Mexican sun, Brazil faced Italy in a memorable World Cup final. It was not just the 4–1 win, it was the 86th-minute goal of Brazil's Carlos Alberto from a Pelé pass that made the world swoon.

Pelé, Tostao, Jairzinho, Roberto Rivelino, Carlos Alberto Torres, Gérson.

Hungary national team
 1953

The "Golden Team" inflicted notable defeats on England, Uruguay and the Soviet Union in three matches that became known as the "Match of the Century," "Battle of Berne" and "Miracle of Berne."

Ferenc Puskás, Sándor Kocsis, Nándor Hidegkuti, Zoltán Czibor, József Bozsik.

Spain national team
2008–2012

While Spanish clubs excelled, the national team had lagged since 1964. But in 2008 they won the Euro final, then the 2010 World Cup and 2012 European Championship – the first team to win successive titles.

Xavi, Andres Iniésta, Cesc Fábregas, David Villa, Fernando Torres.

FC Barcelona
2009

In 2009, Barcelona won every trophy possible: Copa del Rey, La Liga, Champions League, Spanish Supercup, European Supercup and World Cup. It was Pep Guardiola's first year as club coach.

Yaya Touré, Xavi, Andrés Iniesta, Thierry Henry, Lionel Messi, Samuel Eto'o.

AC Milan
1998–1999

In the doldrums since 1979, Milan claimed the Italian title, European Cup, Super Cup and South American Cup during this season after taking on coach Arrigo Sacchi and his "collective intelligence" concept.

Marco van Basten, Frank Rijkaard, Ruud Gullit, Carlo Ancelotti, Paolo Maldini.

Manchester United FC
1998–1999

In this season, Man U won the treble: the Premier League, FA Cup and Champions League. It was the first club to do so. Under manager Alex Ferguson, the team had a 33-game unbeaten streak.

Teddy Sheringham, David Beckham, Ole Gunnar Solskjaer, Dwight Yorke.

Team USA women's squad
 1991

"The Stars and Stripes" team won the first Women's World Cup in 1991. It defeated Norway 2–1 in China after Michelle Aker's goal in the final moments. Their perfect run attracted little attention stateside.

Michelle Akers, Carin Jennings, April Heinrichs, Mia Hamm, Brandi Chastain.

Santos FC
1962–1963

The saying at the time was: "He who has Pelé, rules the roost," and in 1962 Pelé was with the Brazilian team Santos. In these seasons they twice won the Copa Liberatores and the Intercontinental Cup.

Pelé, Gilmar Coultinho, Zito, Pepe, Toninho Guerreiro.

Real Madrid
1956–1960

The UEFA Champions League was established in 1955, and the first five victories were claimed by Real Madrid. The Spanish club's goal total over these five campaigns was a staggering 112!

Alfredo di Stéfano, Francisco Gento, Ferenc Puskás, Raymond Kopa, Hector Rial.

Arsenal FC
2003–2004

Under manager Arsene Wenger, this London team was undefeated in a 49-game season. It earned them the "Invincibles" moniker and the Premier League title. This amazing winning streak has never been repeated.

Thierry Henry, Gilberto Silva, Sol Campbell, Patrick Vieira, Kolo Toure, Robert Pires.

A Moment in Time

Overhead kick

Juventus v. Real Madrid

April 3, 2018

Allianz Stadium, Turin, Italy

Quarter final first leg, Champions League

Having already scored a goal in the 3rd minute, Cristiano Ronaldo performed a spectacular bicycle kick in the 64th minute. It was not just the athleticism of the kick into the top right corner of the net but its height. Ronaldo's foot was in line with the top of the goal. Even Juventus fans stood to cheer.

Controversy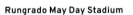

Maradona – the bad and the very good

Argentina v. England

June 22, 1986

Estadio Azteca, Mexico City, Mexico

Quarter finals, 1986 FIFA World Cup

Argentina–England rivalry was already strong, but after Maradona's hand-ball goal in the 51st minute, it reached new heights. Maradona called it the "Hand of God" goal. Then, four minutes later, his genius showed when he dribbled past five England players and the goalkeeper to score the "Goal of the Century."

Sporting Arenas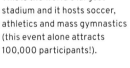

Rungrado May Day Stadium

This is the world's largest stadium and it hosts soccer, athletics and mass gymnastics (this event alone attracts 100,000 participants!).

 114,000　 1989　 Pyongyang, North Korea

Bramall Lane

The oldest major professional football stadium in the world is Bramall Lane. It was originally home to Yorkshire Cricket Club and is now home to Sheffield United FC.

 32,702　 1855　 Sheffield, UK

White Hart Lane

This "new" White Hart Lane for UK's Tottenham Hotspur FC, meant to be ready for the 2018/19 season, is the world's most advanced, with full wireless connectivity and retractable pitch.

 61,000　2018/19　Tottenham, London, UK

FOOTBALL

This contact sport was first played in 1869. It evolved from rugby and association football. National Football League (NFL) games attract the highest attendances of any professional sport in the world. "The Father of American Football," Walter Camp, developed rules that turned a highly defensive (blocking) game into a more physical one. In 1904 there were 18 deaths among players. Then-President Roosevelt threated to ban the sport unless rules were changed. From a team's roster of 53 offense, defense and special play players, only 11 are on the field at one time. The aim is to score the most points from touchdowns, conversions and field goals.

> "Football is like life – it requires perseverance, self-denial, hard work, sacrifice, dedication and respect for authority."
>
> Vince Lombardi (1913–1970), US player and coach

All-Stars

Jerry Rice

1976–1997 · USA

Rice was a wide receiver, regarded as the best ever. He played 20 seasons and won three Super Bowls with the San Francisco 49ers. Rice holds over 100 NFL records, including 197 career receiving touchdowns!

Joe Montana

1973–1995 · USA

When it comes to quarterbacks, Montana tops many lists. He played for 16 seasons (14 with the 49ers), and won four Super Bowls. Like Jerry Rice, he was elected to the Pro Football Hall of Fame in 2000.

Tom Brady

1998– · USA

This quarterback won five Super Bowls with the New England Patriots, for whom he still plays. He holds a record four Super Bowl MVP (Most Valuable Player) awards, and has never had a losing season as a starting quarterback.

Record Breakers

NFL quarterback passing yard* leaders

👤	🔄	📚
Peyton Manning	1998–2015	71,940
Brett Favre	1991–2010	71,838
Drew Brees	2001–	70,445
Tom Brady	2000–	66,159
Dan Marino	1983–1999	61,361

*Passing yard: number of yards obtained on completed passes. All stats on this page current to end 2017.

NFL rushing yard* leaders

👤	🔄	📚
Emmitt Smith	1990–2004	18,355
Walter Payton	1975–1987	16,726
Barry Sanders	1989–1998	15,269
Curtis Martin	1995–2005	14,101
Frank Gore	2005–	14,026

*Rushing yard: number of yards gained by an offensive team as a result of running the ball.

NFL receiving yard* leaders

👤	🔄	📚
Jerry Rice	1985–2004	22,895
Terrell Owens	1996–2010	15,934
Larry Fitzgerald	2004–	15,545
Randy Moss	1998–2012	15,292
Isaac Bruce	1994–2009	15,208

*Receiving yard: number of yards gained by a receiver on a passing play. Yardage includes the distance ball was passed.

NFL interception* leaders

👤	🔄	📚
Paul Krause	1964–1979	81
Emlen Tunnell	1948–1961	79
Rod Woodson	1987–2003	71
Dick Lane	1952–1965	68
Ken Riley	1969–1983	65
Charles Woodson	1998–2012	65

*Interception: when a player catches (intercepts) a forward pass from the opposing team, taking possession. This team will then try to get as much yardage as possible.

Most NFL player appearances*

👤	🔄	✔
Morten Andersen	1982–2007	382
Gary Anderson	1982–2004	353
Jeff Feagles	1988–2009	352
George Blanda	1949–1975	340
Adam Vinatieri	1996–	337
Jason Hanson	1992–2012	327
Jerry Rice	1985–2004	303
John Carney	1988–2010	302
Brett Favre	1991–2010	302
John Kasay	1991–2011	301

*Appearances: only games played in regular season are counted.

NFL quarterback touchdown pass* leaders

👤	🔄	📚
Peyton Manning	1998–2015	539
Brett Favre	1991–2010	508
Tom Brady	2000–	488
Drew Brees	2001–	488
Dan Marino	1983–1999	420
Philip Rivers	2004–	342
Fran Tarkenton	1971–1978	342

*Touchdown pass: a pass to a receiver who makes a touchdown (ball crosses the opponent's goal line).

NFL rushing touchdowns* leaders

👤	🔄	📚
Emmitt Smith	1990–2004	164
LaDainian Tomlinson	2001–2011	145
Marcus Allen	1982–1997	123
Walter Payton	1975–1987	110
Jim Brown	1957–1965	106

*Rushing touchdown: touchdown scored by a player after receiving a hand-off (ball handed not passed).

NFL receiving touchdown* leaders

👤	🔄	📚
Jerry Rice	1985–2004	197
Randy Moss	1998–2012	156
Terrell Owens	1996–2010	153
Cris Carter	1987–2002	130
Marvin Harrison	1996–2008	128

*Receiving touchdown: a touchdown after catching the ball in the end zone or from a pass. Both players are given credit.

NFL tackle* leaders

👤	🔄	📚
Bruce Smith	1985–2003	200
Reggie White	1985–2000	198
Kevin Greene	1985–1997	160
Julius Peppers	2002–	155
Chris Doleman	1985–1998	151

*Tackle: a physical action by one player that causes the tackled player (holding the ball) to touch the ground with a part of his body other than legs and feet. The purpose is to stop forward play or a player going out of bounds.

Leading NFL Super Bowl coach record

👤	🏆	🥈
Bill Belichick	5	2
Don Shula	2	4
Tom Landry	2	3
Chuck Noll	4	0
Joe Gibbs	3	1
Bud Grant	0	4
Marv Levy	0	4
Dan Reeves	0	4
Bill Walsh	3	0
Bill Parcells	2	1
Mike Holmgren	1	2

Football

▼ National Football League

This professional football league consists of 32 teams – 16 from the National Football Conference (NFC) and 16 from the American Football Conference (AFC). It has a 17-week season. After each team plays 16 games, six teams (including two wild cards) from each conference play for a spot in the Super Bowl. The Super Bowl, held on the first Sunday in February, is between the NFC and AFC champions.

Current teams of the NFL

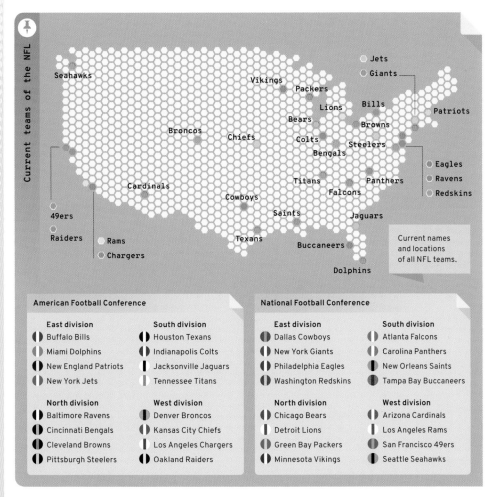

Current names and locations of all NFL teams.

American Football Conference

East division
- Buffalo Bills
- Miami Dolphins
- New England Patriots
- New York Jets

South division
- Houston Texans
- Indianapolis Colts
- Jacksonville Jaguars
- Tennessee Titans

North division
- Baltimore Ravens
- Cincinnati Bengals
- Cleveland Browns
- Pittsburgh Steelers

West division
- Denver Broncos
- Kansas City Chiefs
- Los Angeles Chargers
- Oakland Raiders

National Football Conference

East division
- Dallas Cowboys
- New York Giants
- Philadelphia Eagles
- Washington Redskins

South division
- Atlanta Falcons
- Carolina Panthers
- New Orleans Saints
- Tampa Bay Buccaneers

North division
- Chicago Bears
- Detroit Lions
- Green Bay Packers
- Minnesota Vikings

West division
- Arizona Cardinals
- Los Angeles Rams
- San Francisco 49ers
- Seattle Seahawks

Super Bowl championship records*

	🏆	2	📅★
Pittsburgh Steelers	6	2	2009
New England Patriots	5	5	2017
Dallas Cowboys	5	3	1996
San Francisco 49ers	5	1	1995
Green Bay Packers	4	1	2011
New York Giants	4	1	2012
Denver Broncos	3	5	2016
Oakland Raiders	3	2	1984
Washington Redskins	3	2	1992
Miami Dolphins	2	3	1974
Indianapolis Colts	2	2	2007
Baltimore Ravens	2	0	2013
Los Angeles Rams	1	2	2000
Seattle Seahawks	1	2	2014
Philadelphia Eagles	1	2	2018
Kansas City Chiefs	1	1	1970
Chicago Bears	1	1	1986
New York Jets	1	0	1969
Tampa Bay Buccaneers	1	0	2003
New Orleans Saints	1	0	2010
Minnesota Vikings	0	4	
Buffalo Bills	0	4	
Cincinnati Bengals	0	2	
Atlanta Falcons	0	2	
Carolina Panthers	0	2	
Los Angeles Chargers	0	1	
Tennessee Titans	0	1	
Arizona Cardinals	0	1	

* List covers Super Bowl 1967–2018 and teams' current names, and excludes teams no longer in operation or without Super Bowl exposure.

Scoring records at a Super Bowl, single team

	🏆	🏈
Most points		
San Francisco 49ers	XXIV	55
Most consecutive points		
Washington Redskins	XXII	42
Most points by a losing team		
New England Patriots	LII	33
Fewest points		
Miami Dolphins	VI	3
Fewest points by a winning team		
Miami Dolphins	VII	14
Most points scored in any quarter* of play		
Washington Redskins	XXII	35

* **Quarter:** four quarters of 15 minutes make up the 60-minute game. There is a two-minute break after 1st and 3rd quarters, and 12 minutes after the 2nd, which is half time.

Combined scoring records at a Super Bowl

	🏈
Most points scored (Super Bowl XXIV)*	
San Francisco 49ers	49
San Diego Chargers	26
Fewest points scored (Super Bowl VII)	
Miami Dolphins	14
Washington Redskins	7

* The second highest combined Super Bowl final score is 74 and this occurred in 2018 (Super Bowl LII) between the New England Patriots (33) and the Philadelphia Eagles (41).

Touchdown records at a Super Bowl, single team

	🏆	🙌
Most touchdowns		
San Francisco 49ers	XXIV	8
Fewest touchdowns		
Miami Dolphins	VI	0

Factfile

🥇 Vince Lombardi Trophy

Vince Lombardi won two Super Bowls (1967, 1968) with the Green Bay Packers and five NFL championships. Lombardi died suddenly in 1970 and the name of the Super Bowl trophy was changed to honor his legacy.

⭐ Pittsburgh Steelers

This Pennsylvania team has won the championship more times than any other team, playing in 8 Super Bowls. The glory year was 1974 when coach Chuck Noll drafted Lynn Swann, Jack Lambert, John Stallworth and Mike Webster, who all became Hall of Famers.

Canadian Football League `CFL`

The highest professional football league in Canada consists of nine teams based in nine cities – four from the East division and five from the West division. First started in 1958 (with rules that differ slightly from the NFL), the league's 21-week regular season (June to early November) is followed by a three-week single-elimination playoff, culminating in the championship match between the top team from each division. The winner receives the Grey Cup.

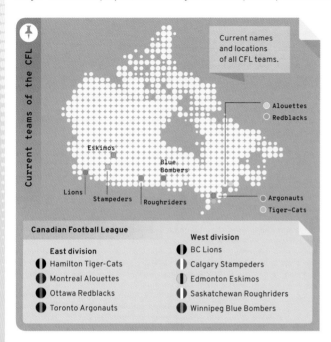

Current names and locations of all CFL teams.

Canadian Football League

East division	West division
Hamilton Tiger-Cats	BC Lions
Montreal Alouettes	Calgary Stampeders
Ottawa Redblacks	Edmonton Eskimos
Toronto Argonauts	Saskatchewan Roughriders
	Winnipeg Blue Bombers

Multiple Grey Cup winners

	🏆	🥈
Active teams		
Toronto Argonauts	17	6
Edmonton Eskimos	14	9
Winnipeg Blue Bombers	10	14
Hamilton Tiger-Cats	8	12
Montreal Alouettes	7	11
Calgary Stampeders	7	9
BC Lions	6	4
Saskatchewan Roughriders	4	15
Defunct or amateur teams*		
Ottawa Rough Riders	9	6
Hamilton Tigers	5	3
University of Toronto Varsity Blues	4	2
Queen's University	3	0
Toronto Balmy Beach	2	2
Sarnia Imperials	2	1

*These teams are no longer in the CFL, but they did win multiple Grey Cups when operational.

Factfile

 Grey Cup

This is the second-oldest North American trophy after hockey's Stanley Cup, and it is awarded to the CFL champion. It was made in 1909 for the amateur hockey champions, but ended up being used for football. The cup was stolen twice and held for ransom.

Toronto Argonauts

The oldest surviving team – and without a name change – in the CFL, they dominate the Grey Cup chart of winners. But between 1953 and 1982, they suffered a 30-year slump – not even taking a place in the final two. These "dark ages" ended with a win in 1983.

X-League

This is the top-level professional football league in Japan. It was founded in 1971, and like its North American equivalent, it is divided into divisions: East, West and Central. There are 52 company and club teams. (Company teams consist of players employed by the sponsoring company.) The season culminates with the Japan X Bowl (JXB) final.

Japan X Bowl* team records

	🏆	🥈
Obic Seagulls	8	2
Panasonic Impulse	7	7
Asahi Beer Silver Star	4	4
Fujitsu Frontiers	3	6
Onward Skylarks	3	3
Lixil Deers	2	4
Asahi Soft Drink Challengers	2	0
Renown Rovers	2	0
Elecom Kobe Finies	0	2
IBM BigBlue	0	2
NEC Falcons	0	1

* Japan X Bowl champions compete for the Rice Bowl against college Koshien Bowl champions.

With the Fujitsu Frontiers, running back Gino Gordon won the 2014 MVP award (the first American to do so) and was an All-X-League member three times.

Factfile

 Record JXB final
Fujitsu Frontiers v. IBM BigBlue

In the 2017 final, the Frontiers set JXB points and winning margin records, beating BigBlue 63–23. The Frontiers' opening 99-yard return kickoff for a touchdown set the scene for the whole game.

 Obic Seagulls

The most successful team in Japan has won the Rice Bowl seven times and the JXB eight times. Over 26 seasons and 180 games, this club team has had 144 wins, 33 losses and three draws.

Arena Football League   `AFL`

AFL is an indoor professional football league. Played in an arena on a padded surface that is about a quarter the size of an NFL field, it debuted at Madison Square Garden in 1981. At one time there were 19 teams, but no longer. There are eight players on the field, and a standard sized football is used in this fast-paced, offensive-play game.

ArenaBowl champions

	🏆	🥈
Arizona Rattlers	5	5
Tampa Bay Storm	5	3
Detroit Drive	4	2
San Jose SaberCats	4	1
Philadelphia Soul	3	2
Orlando Predators	2	5
Jacksonville Sharks	1	1
Denver Dynamite	1	0
Albany Firebirds	1	0
Grand Rapids Rampage	1	0
Colorado Crush	1	0
Chicago Rush	1	0
Spokane Shock	1	0

Arizona Rattlers' Hunkie Cooper twice won Ironman of the Year award and an AFL MVP. Only one other AFL footballer has achieved this.

Factfile

 Foster Trophy

This trophy is presented to the ArenaBowl champions. It is named for AFL founder, Jim Foster. The 28-inch-tall column is engraved with the phrase, "Character, Excellence, Commitment and Teamwork."

 Philadelphia Soul

Rock star Jon Bon Jovi was a 2003 founder of this team. They were ArenaBowl champions in 2008, 2016 and 2017. In the 2017 final, Soul came back from a record 20–7 deficit to win.

Super Teams

Chicago Bears
 1985

This talented team under coach Mike "Iron Man" Ditka had only one defeat in this season and went on to win its ninth NFL championship. The secret of its success was the innovative 46 defense formation.

 Jim McMahon, Walter Payton, Mike Singletary, William "Refrigerator" Perry.

★★★☆☆☆☆☆☆☆

Dallas Cowboys
 1992

With the No. 1 ranked defense at the time and the youngest team, the Cowboys defeated the 49ers on their way to beating the Buffalo Bills at Super Bowl XXVII 52–17 – the third-highest scoring Super Bowl.

 Emmitt Smith, Troy Aikman, Michael Irvin, Charles Haley.

★★★★★★★★☆☆

Miami Dolphins
 1972

This squad finished the season undefeated and untied – a first in NFL history – and then went on to win the Super Bowl 14–7 over the Redskins. This "perfect season" was masterminded by coach Don Shula.

 Nick Buoniconti, Larry Csonka, Larry Little, Bob Griese, Jim Langer, Paul Warfield.

★★★★★★★★☆☆

Buffalo Bills
 1991

The Bills lost to the New York Giants in Super Bowl XXV, by one point! If it hadn't been for a missed 47-yard field goal attempt in the last seconds, the Bills would have won. They still haven't won a Super Bowl.

 Bruce Smith, Thurman Thomas, Jim Kelly.

★☆☆☆☆☆☆☆☆☆

New England Patriots
 2007

An undefeated season ended with a surprise 17–14 defeat to the New York Giants in Super Bowl XLII. It is the only team with a regular-season clean slate not to win the Vince Lombardi Trophy.

 Tom Brady, Randy Moss, Wes Welker, Jabar Gaffney, Rodney Harrison.

★★☆☆☆☆☆☆☆☆

Denver Broncos
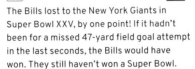 **1999**

Hailed as the 12th-greatest Super Bowl winners ever, this team built on the club's magical Super Bowl XXXII win. They soundly beat the Atlanta Falcons 34–19 in Super Bowl XXXIII.

John Elway, Terrell Davis, Ed McCaffrey, Neil Smith, Shannon Sharpe.

★★★☆☆☆☆☆☆☆

San Francisco 49ers
 1988–1989

This squad had an offense at the peak of its powers and an underestimated defense. In the playoffs it outscored opponents 126–26 and won its fourth Super Bowl under new coach George Seifert.

 Joe Montana, Jerry Rice, Brent Jones, Roger Craig, Tom Rathman.

★★★★★★★★★☆

Washington Redskins
 1991

This Redskin team scored 485 points and conceded the third-lowest number of points in NFL history. They won Super Bowl XXVI against the Buffalo Bills.

Mark Rypien, Ricky Sanders, Earnest Byner, Art Monk, Gary Clark, Ricky Sanders.

★★★★★☆☆☆☆☆

Pittsburgh Steelers
 1979–1980

This team defended its Super Bowl XIV win (defeating the Rams 31–19) to become the only team to win back-to-back Bowls *twice*. It was also the first team to reach the final after posting only nine regular season wins.

 Terry Bradshaw, John Stallworth, Franco Harris, Sidney Thorton, Jack Ham.

★★★★★★★★★☆

Green Bay Packers
 1996

In 1996, the Packers won their third Super Bowl and 12th NFL Championship. Going undefeated at home was a club first, as was having the No. 1 team. In Super Bowl XXXI, they defeated the Patriots.

 Brett Favre, Desmond Howard, Reggie White, Sean Jones.

★★★★★★☆☆☆☆

A Moment in Time

"The Catch"

 San Francisco 49ers v. Dallas Cowboys

 January 10, 1982

Candlestick Park, San Francisco, California

NFC Championship

This play has gone down in history. There were 51 seconds remaining and the score was tied. That is when 49ers wide receiver Dwight Clark caught the ball at the back of the end zone for the winning touchdown. It sent the 49ers to their first Super Bowl after a series of defeats by the Cowboys.

Controversy

"HeadsetGate"

 New England Patriots v. Pittsburgh Steelers

 September 11, 2015

 Gillette Stadium, Foxborough, Massachusetts

NFL season opener

With their reputation in doubt after "Deflategate" (using deflated footballs) and "Spygate" (spying on rival teams), the Patriots were suspected of interfering with the Steelers' headset transmissions. The Steelers coach heard only the Patriots' radio broadcast. It was a Patriots win, but without glory.

Sporting Arenas

Michigan Stadium

The world's second-largest stadium is nicknamed "The Big House." In 2013, it broke records for a college game with a 115,109-strong crowd watching Michigan v. Notre Dame.

👥 107,601   🔨 1927   📍 Ann Arbor, Michigan

Los Angeles Memorial Coliseum

Known for its columned entrance, this stadium is a National Historic Landmark. It hosted the Summer Olympics three times (a record) and its Olympic cauldron is still lit for special events.

👥 78,500   🔨 1923   📍 Los Angeles, California

Mercedes-Benz Superdome

This is the largest fixed-domed structure in the world. The dome measures 680 feet across. In 2005, it housed thousands of locals seeking shelter from Hurricane Katrina.

👥 76,468   🔨 1975   📍 New Orleans, Louisiana

ATHLETICS

Athletics and its track and field athletes have become the star attractions at global sporting competitions. Track includes running and racewalking events that cover distances from 100-meter sprints to 26-mile marathons. Long jump, high jump, triple jump, hurdles, steeplechase, shot put, discus throw, hammer throw and javelin are grouped as field sports. Pentathlons, heptathlons and decathlons, which consist of five, seven and ten events, combine track and field sports. There are 30 major competitions on the athletics calendar, but the most important are the Olympics, Paralympics, World Championships and World Indoor Championships.

> "I told myself: 'Listen: Don't panic. Take your time, chip away, and work your way back in.'"
>
> Usain Bolt, eight-time Olympic champion (2008, 2012, 2016)

All-Stars

Usain Bolt

2001–2016   Jamaica

With eight Olympic golds, and three world records, this Jamaican 11-time World Champion is the greatest sprinter of all time! But Bolt's triple-triple in the 100, 200 and 4x100 meters was lost when a 2008 relay-team member failed a drug test.

Jackie Joyner-Kersee

1979–2000   USA

In heptathlon and long jump, this American amassed six Olympic medals and four World Championship golds, despite having severe asthma. Considered the greatest female athlete ever, her 7,291 heptathlon points is still a record.

Babe Didrikson Zaharias

1930–1956   USA

This American won three Olympic track and field medals in 1932, was an All-American basketballer and excelled in almost every sport. She won 10 major LPGA golf championships and was Athlete of the Year six times.

Record Breakers

Records in men's sprint

100 m Usain Bolt	JAM	9.58
200 m Usain Bolt	JAM	19.19
400 m Wayde van Niekerk	RSA	43.03

Records in men's middle distance

800 m David Rudisha	KEN	1:40.91
1,000 m Noah Ngeny	KEN	2:11.96
1,500 m Hicham El Guerrouj	MAR	3:26.00
Mile Hicham El Guerrouj	MAR	3:43.13

Records in men's long distance

3,000 m Daniel Komen	KEN	7:20.67
5,000 m Kenenisa Bekele	ETH	12:37.35
10,000 m Kenenisa Bekele	ETH	26:17.53
20,000 m Haile Gebrselassie	ETH	56:25.98

Records in men's relay

4×100 m Nesta Carter, Michael Frater, Yohan Blake, Usain Bolt	JAM	36.84
4×400 m Andrew Valmon, Quincy Watts, Butch Reynolds, Michael Johnson	USA	2:54.29

Records in men's hurdling

110-m hurdles Aries Merritt	USA	12.80
400-m hurdles Kevin Young	USA	46.78
3,000-m steeplechase* Saif Saaeed Shaheen	QAT	7:53.63

* **Steeplechase:** in this race, runners have to clear 18–28 barriers (which remain upright if hit) and 5–7 water jumps.

Records in men's marathon*

Half marathon Zersenay Tadese	ERI	58:23
Marathon Dennis Kipruto Kimetto	KEN	2:02:57

* **Marathon:** a long-distance road race (26.2 miles). A half marathon is 13.1 miles.

Records in men's walking races

10 km Paquillo Fernández	ESP	37:53.09
20 km Bernardo Segura	MEX	1:17:25.6
50 km Yohann Diniz	FRA	3:35:27.20

Records in men's jumping events

Long jump Mike Powell	USA	8.95 m
Triple jump Jonathan Edwards	GBR	18.29 m
High jump Javier Sotomayor	CUB	2.45 m
Pole vault Renaud Lavillenie	FRA	6.16 m

Records in men's throwing events

Shot put Randy Barnes	USA	23.12 m
Discus throw Jürgen Schult	GDR	74.08 m
Javelin throw Jan Železný	CZE	98.48 m
Hammer throw Yuriy Sedykh	URS	86.74 m

Record total points in the decathlon*

Ashton Eaton	USA	9,045

* **Decathlon:** a combined track and field event consisting of 10 sports: 100-, 400- and 1,500-meter races; long and high jump; shot put; pole vault; javelin throw; hurdles; and discus. The winners are determined by the total of all points earned in each discipline. The highest total wins.

Ashton Eaton was the second athlete to break the 9,000 points barrier. He also holds the world record (6,645 points) in indoor men's heptathlon.

Records in women's sprint

100 m		
Florence Griffith Joyner	USA	10.49
200 m		
Florence Griffith Joyner	USA	21.34
400 m		
Marita Koch	GDR	47.60

Records in women's middle distance

800 m		
Jarmila Kratochvílová	TCH	1:53.28
1,000 m		
Svetlana Masterkova	RUS	2:28.98
1,500 m		
Genzebe Dibaba	ETH	3:50.07
Mile		
Svetlana Masterkova	RUS	4:12.56

Records in women's long distance

3,000 m		
Wang Junxia	CHN	8:06.11
5,000 m		
Tirunesh Dibaba	ETH	14:11.15
10,000 m		
Almaz Ayana	ETH	29:17.45
20,000 m		
Tegla Loroupe	KEN	1:05:26.6

Records in women's relay

4×100 m		
Tianna Madison	USA	40.82
Allyson Felix		
Bianca Knight		
Carmelita Jeter		
4×400 m		
Tatyana Ledovskaya	URS	3:15.17
Olga Nazarova		
Mariya Pinigina		
Olga Bryzgina		

Records in women's hurdling

100-m hurdles		
Kendra Harrison	USA	12.20
400-m hurdles		
Yuliya Pechonkina	RUS	52.34
3,000-m steeplechase*		
Ruth Jebet	BRN	8:52.78

* See page 14.

Records in women's marathon*

Half marathon		
Joyciline Jepkosgei	KEN	1:04.51
Marathon		
Paula Radcliffe	GBR	2:15.25

* Marathon: a long-distance road race (26.2 miles). A half marathon is 13.1 miles.

Records in women's walking races

10 km		
Nadezhda Ryashkina	URS	41:56.23
20 km		
Olimpiada Ivanova	RUS	1:26:52.3
50 km (road)		
Liang Rui	CHN	4:04:36

Records in women's jumping events

Long jump		
Galina Chistyakova	URS	7.52 m
Triple jump		
Inessa Kravets	UKR	15.50 m
High jump		
Stefka Kostadinova	BUL	2.09 m
Pole vault		
Yelena Isinbayeva	RUS	5.06 m

Records in women's throwing events

Shot put		
Natalya Lisovskaya	URS	22.63 m
Discus throw		
Gabriele Reinsch	GDR	76.80 m
Javelin throw		
Barbora Špotáková	CZE	72.28 m
Hammer throw		
Anita Włodarczyk	POL	82.98 m

Record points in the heptathlon*

Jackie Joyner-Kersee	USA	7,291

* Heptathlon: a combined event in athletics consisting of seven track and field events: 100-, 200- and 800-meter races; high and long jumps; shot put and javelin throw. The winners are determined by the total of all points earned in each discipline. The highest total wins.

In major competitions, women compete in heptathlon, but there is a women's decathlon world record (8,366 points) held by Lithuanian Austra Skujyté.

A Moment in Time

The spirit of the Olympics

 Derek Redmond

📅	August 3, 1992
📍	Estadi Olímpic de Montjuïc, Barcelona, Spain
↖	Olympic semifinal 400-meter sprint

Seconds into the race, Derek Redmond's hamstring snapped, but the British athlete got to his feet. He ignored officials and limped the course. His father fended off security and helped his son to the finish to a standing ovation from the 65,000-strong crowd. Though disqualified, Redmond became a hero.

Controversy

A comeback fails

 Ben Johnson

📅	June 12, 1999
📍	Kitchener, Ontario, Canada
↖	Track meet, 100 meters

When disgraced Canadian sprinter Ben Johnson got to the starting blocks for this race he was the lone runner – no one would compete with him for fear of tainting their reputation, so his 11-second race was against the clock. (His rescinded 1987 World Record was 9.83.) Within months, his life ban for doping was reinstated.

Sporting Arenas

Beijing National Stadium
Known as the Bird's Nest because of its shape and "woven" trusses, it was used for the 2008 Summer Olympics and Paralympics. It is also to be a venue for the 2022 Winter Games.

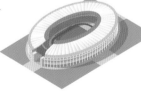

👥 80,000 📐 2007 📍 Beijing, China

Olympiastadion
It was here in 1936 that Adolf Hitler refused to congratulate black US athlete Jesse Owens on his four gold medals. Here, in 2009, Usain Bolt broke his own 100-meter World Record by 0.11 seconds.

👥 74,475 📐 1936 📍 Berlin, Germany

Panathenaic Stadium
Built of marble, it hosted the opening and closing ceremonies and four events of the first modern Olympics (1896). In 2004, it was the venue for Olympic archery and the marathon finish.

👥 45,000 📐 600-501 BCE 📍 Athens, Greece

Focus on the Olympics

Athletics has been part of every modern Games since 1896. (There was even a footrace at the first games in 776 BCE.) In the early 1900s, tug-of-war was an Olympic event! Currently there are 48 athletic medal events up for grabs at an Olympics. Jamaica might only have competed in its first Olympics in 1948 (the US's was in 1896), but Jamaica is currently eighth in the all-time medal table.

Individual athletes with five or more gold medals

			●	●	●	○
Men						
Paavo Nurmi	1920–1934	FIN	9	3	0	12
Carl Lewis	1979–1997	USA	9	1	0	10
Usain Bolt	2002–2017	JAM	8	0	0	8
Ray Ewry	1900–1908	USA	8	0	0	8
Ville Ritola	1921–1928	FIN	5	3	0	8
Women						
Allyson Felix	2004–	USA	6	3	0	9

Most appearances at Olympic Games

			✓	●	●	●	○
Men							
Jesús Ángel García Bragado	ESP	1992–2016	7	0	0	0	0
Women							
Merlene Ottey	JAM	1980–2004	7	0	3	6	9

Of its total 77 Olympic medals, 76 of Jamaica's have been won in athletics, and most of those were in track events. The 77th medal was a bronze in cycling in 1980.

All-time athletics medal table, by country

	●	●	●	○
USA	335	259	207	801
Soviet Union URS	64	55	74	193
GBR	55	80	68	203
Finland	48	36	30	114
East Germany GDR	38	36	35	109
Kenya	30	37	26	93
Poland	25	18	14	57
Jamaica	22	33	21	76
Ethiopia	22	10	21	53
Australia	21	26	26	73
Russia	21	19	20	60
Sweden	19	21	41	81
Italy	19	15	26	60
Germany	18	24	38	80
France	14	26	29	69
Canada	14	15	31	60
West Germany FRG	12	14	17	43
Romania	11	14	10	35
Czechoslovakia TCH	11	8	5	24

Factfile

 Merlene "Bronze Queen" Ottey

This Jamaican sprinter won nine Olympic medals and was her country's first female medalist, but none of her medals were gold! She came close in the 1996 games, but a photo finish for gold was awarded to the US. Ottey competed until 2012, at age 52.

 The Emperor and the Gentleman
Haile Gebrselassie v. Paul Tergat

At the 2000 Olympics, the Ethiopian "Emperor" Gebrselassie and the Kenyan "Gentleman" Tergat lined up for the 10,000-meter finals. Tergat had a small lead with 250 meters to go, but Gebrselassie powered up to win the 27-minute race by just 0.09 seconds!

World Championships in Athletics

IAAF

Founded in 1912, the International Association of Athletic Federations (IAAF) organizes competitions like the World Championships, sets the rules and authorizes world records. The IAAF also ensures that there are facilities and opportunities for everyone to participate in athletics. The championships, which started in 1976, take place every two years, and like the Olympics, are a premier athletics meet.

Individual athletes with five or more gold medals

		●	●	●	○
Men					
Usain Bolt	JAM	11	2	1	14
LaShawn Merritt	USA	8	3	0	11
Carl Lewis	USA	8	1	1	10
Michael Johnson	USA	8	0	0	8
Mo Farah	GBR	6	2	0	8
Sergey Bubka*	URS/UKR	6	0	0	6
Jeremy Wariner	USA	5	1	0	6
Kenenisa Bekele	ETH	5	0	1	6
Lars Riedel	GER	5	0	1	6
Women					
Allyson Felix	USA	11	3	2	16
Shelly-Ann Fraser-Pryce	JAM	7	2	0	9
Gail Devers	USA	5	3	0	8
Sanya Richards-Ross	USA	5	2	0	7
Tirunesh Dibaba	ETH	5	1	0	6
Natasha Hastings	USA	5	1	0	6

* **Sergey Bubka**: representing the Soviet Union (to 1991) and then Ukraine, he won the pole vault in each of the six championships he competed in.

All-time athletics medal table, by country

	●	●	●	○
USA	155	106	91	352
Kenya	55	48	37	140
Russia	47	54	50	151
Germany	36	35	43	114
Jamaica	32	44	39	115
GBR	28	33	38	99
Ethiopia	27	25	25	77
Soviet Union URS	23	27	28	78
Cuba	21	23	13	57
East Germany GDR	21	19	16	56
Poland	17	14	22	53
China	15	21	17	53
Czech Republic	14	6	5	25
France	13	17	22	52
South Africa	12	6	9	27
Italy	11	15	17	43
Australia	11	14	10	35
Ukraine	11	11	15	37
Belarus	10	13	12	35
Morocco	10	12	7	29

Factfile

 Allyson Felix

Felix is the only female athlete to have won six Olympic golds! This American sprinter (100, 200 and 400 meters and 100- and 400-meter relay) also tops the World Championships table with 16 medals. Felix has won the Jesse Owens Athlete of the Year five times.

 Team USA

Team USA dominates the athletic World Championships, leading the runner-up, Kenya, by 100 gold medals. This team has set the greatest number of world records (10). Among the team's many stars, Carl Lewis broke three world records and Michael Johnson, two.

Mile run `IAAF`

This is classed as a middle-distance race. Though all other athletic events are in metric, this 1,760-yard race is in a class of its own. Lining up to do a best time on outdoor or indoor tracks (there are records for both) are amateurs and top professionals alike. The first mile world record (4:14.4) was set in 1913 by American John Paul Jones.

All-time best mile times*

Men		
Hicham El Guerrouj	MAR	3:43.13
Noah Ngeny	KEN	3:43.40
Noureddine Morceli	ALG	3:44.39
Steve Cram	GBR	3:46.32
Daniel Komen	KEN	3:46.38
Vénuste Niyongabo	BUR	3:46.70
Saïd Aouita	MAR	3:46.76
Women		
Svetlana Masterkova	RUS	4:12.56
Genzebe Dibaba	ETH	4:13.31
Paula Ivan	ROM	4:15.61
Natalya Artyomova	URS	4:15.80
Hellen Obiri	KEN	4:16.56
Mary Slaney	USA	4:16.71
Faith Kipyegon	KEN	4:16.71

* **Times**: record times on outdoor tracks.

Factfile

Roger Bannister

It was at the Iffley Road Track, Oxford, UK, on May 6, 1954, that this British runner ran the first-ever sub-four-minute mile. The track was renamed in his honor. Bannister died in 2018.

Hicham El Guerrouj

The greatest middle-distance runner, this Moroccan retains world records in 1,500-meter, mile and outdoor 2,000-meter events. His career gold medal tally is nine. He retired in 2006.

World Cross Country Championships `IAAF`

Currently this premier cross-country event is held every two years. The course is over natural terrain and can include hills, woodlands, mud and a water jump. Until 2017 when a mixed gender 4x400-meter relay was added, there was one race for senior men (10–12 km) and one for senior women (8–10 km). The competition to win is furious!

Athletes with most gold medals

Men		
Kenenisa Bekele	ETH	6
Paul Tergat	KEN	5
John Ngugi	KEN	5
Women		
Grete Waitz	NOR	5

Teams* with most medals, by gold

	●	●	●	○
Men				
Kenya	24	5	3	32
Ethiopia	10	13	7	30
Women				
Kenya	12	10	2	24
Ethiopia	11	12	1	24

* **Teams**: the top six places of the national men's and the national women's teams are totaled. The team with the lowest total wins gold.

Factfile

Kenya

From 1986–2003, the men's team won the world title 18 times in a row! It is one of the longest winning streaks in sports history. Team heroes included John Ngugi, Paul Kipkoech and Paul Tergat.

The ending no one expected
Ethiopia v. Kenya

In the 2007 World Championships, Kenya cheered when an Ethiopian was overcome by heat. The Kenyans went wild expecting a home win. But the Kenyan was pipped to the line by an Eritrean.

World Triathlon Series `ITU`

At the end of eight competition rounds, the Grand Final race determines the world champion in this grueling sport. The elite race consists of a 1.5-km open water swim followed by a 40-km cycle and a 10-km run. It tests a triathlete's endurance across the three disciplines. First started in 1989, Australia currently tops the medal table with 19 golds.

Athletes with most gold medals

Men		
Javier Gómez	ESP	5
Simon Lessing	GBR	4
Peter Robertson	AUS	3
Mario Mola	ESP	2
Alistair Brownlee	GBR	2
Women		
Emma Snowsill	AUS	3
Michellie Jones	AUS	2
Emma Carney	AUS	2
Gwen Jorgensen	USA	2
Karen Smyers	USA	2
Flora Duffy	BER	2
Helen Jenkins	GBR	2
Emma Moffatt	AUS	2

Average triathlon times: 10-km run, 55–60 mins; 40-km cycle, 80 mins; 1.5-km swim, 40 mins.

Factfile

Javier Gómez

This Spanish triathlete has won the Grand Final five times. Though a heart problem took him off the circuit for a while, he achieved 54 top-10 places in 57 events. In the 2012 Olympic event, he won silver.

Alistair Brownlee
Jonathan Brownlee

Alistair has two Olympic golds, and brother Jonathan a silver and bronze. Both have multiple ITU medals. In Mexico 2016, Alistair aided his exhausted brother in the final meters, pushing him over the line.

Para Athletics

At the 1960 Paralympics there were approximately 400 para athletes competing in 25 track and field medal events; in 2020, 1,100 para athletes will compete in 168 medal events. Depending on the impairment, athletes may use wheelchairs, tandems, handcycles or prosthetics, and those with visual impairments may use a sighted guide.

Top Paralympic athletes, by gold

		●	●	●	○
Men					
Franz Nietlispach	SUI	14	6	2	22
Bart Dodson	USA	13	3	4	20
Heinz Frei	SUI	11	6	5	22
Tim Sullivan	AUS	10	0	0	10
Women					
Chantal Petitclerc	CAN	14	5	2	21
Purificacíon Santamarta	ESP	11	4	1	16
Tanni Grey-Thompson	GBR	11	4	1	16
Zipora Rubin-Rosenbaum	ISR	11	3	5	19

The current para World Record for the 100 meters is 10.46 seconds and is held by Jason Smyth, a blind sprinter. For comparison, Usain Bolt's record is 9.58.

Superstar ★

Chantal Petitclerc

This wheelchair athlete made her Paralympic debut in Barcelona 1992, and competed in four further games. She ended her career in Beijing in 2008 by winning every track event from 100 meters to 1,500 meters for a second time and breaking many world records.

1992–2008   ⚑ Canada

Para Athletes

BASEBALL

Though the first organized game was held in Canada in 1838, baseball's heartland is in the United States. Here, in 1845, the game's first rules were compiled, and by the 1850s there was a national league. By 1878 it had been exported, taking deepest root in Japan and the Caribbean. Baseball's fans now number 500 million! Played by two teams, the aim is to score maximum runs when batting and to prevent runs when pitching and fielding. To play, you need a round bat, a ball and catcher's mitt, and four bases (home, 1st, 2nd and 3rd) placed on the corners of a square with 90-foot sides. Beyond this infield and inside the foul lines is the outfield.

> **"They give you a round bat and they throw you a round ball. And they tell you to hit it square."**
>
> Willie "Pops" Stargell (1940–2001), left fielder and first baseman

All-Stars

Mike Trout

🔄 2011–   🏳 USA

Nicknamed the "Millville Meteor," this center fielder is rated as baseball's No. 1 player. Since joining the Los Angeles Angels, he has racked up six MLB All-Star appearances and two American League MVP awards.

Barry Lamar Bonds

🔄 1986–2007   🏳 USA

Bonds holds the record for the second-most seasons (eight) with 40+ home runs in MLB and has seven National League MVP awards and 14 All-Star selections. His hitting is exceptional; his outfield work got him eight Gold Gloves.

Babe Ruth

🔄 1914–1935   🏳 USA

Decades pass, but the "Sultan of Swat" reigns supreme. America's first sports superstar was a seven-time World Series champion and twice selected for the MLB All-Stars. His number 3 shirt was retired by the New York Yankees.

Record Breakers

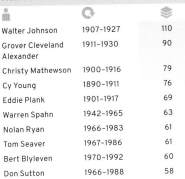

MLB career base hits* leaders

👤	🔄	⬚
Pete Rose	1963–1986	4,256
Ty Cobb	1905–1928	4,191
Hank Aaron	1954–1976	3,771
Stan Musial	1941–1963	3,630
Tris Speaker	1907–1928	3,514
Derek Jeter	1995–2014	3,465
Honus Wagner	1897–1917	3,430
Carl Yastrzemski	1961–1983	3,419
Paul Molitor	1978–1998	3,319
Eddie Collins	1906–1930	3,314

* **Base hits (H):** number of times in an MLB career that a batter reached first base after hitting the ball into fair territory without error or fielder's choice.

MLB career times on base* leaders

👤	🔄	⬚
Pete Rose	1963–1986	5,929
Barry Bonds	1986–2007	5,599
Ty Cobb	1905–1928	5,532
Rickey Henderson	1979–2003	5,343
Carl Yastrzemski	1961–1983	5,304

* **Times on base (TOB):** total times a batter during MLB career has reached base as a result of hits, walks and hit by pitches.

MLB career home run* leaders

👤	🔄	⬚
Barry Bonds	1986–2007	762
Hank Aaron	1954–1976	755
Babe Ruth	1914–1935	714
Alex Rodriguez	1994–2016	696
Willie Mays	1951–1973	660
Albert Pujols	2001–	632
Ken Griffey Jr.	1989–2010	630
Jim Thome	1991–2012	612
Sammy Sosa	1989–2007	609
Frank Robinson	1956–1976	586

* **Home run (HR):** a hit that allows the batter to circle the bases and reach home safely in one play. Totals relate only to a player's MLB career.

MLB career strikeout* leaders (batters)

👤	🔄	⬚
Reggie Jackson	1967–1985	2,597
Jim Thome	1991–2012	2,548
Adam Dunn	2001–2014	2,379
Sammy Sosa	1989–2007	2,306
Alex Rodriguez	1994–2016	2,287
Andrés Galarraga	1985–2004	2,003
Jose Canseco	1985–2001	1,942
Willie Stargell	1962–1982	1,936
Mike Cameron	1995–2011	1,901
Mike Schmidt	1972–1989	1,883

* **Strikeout (K or SO):** this occurs when the batter receives three strikes during a time at bat. It usually means that the batter is out.

MLB career shutout* leaders

👤	🔄	⬚
Walter Johnson	1907–1927	110
Grover Cleveland Alexander	1911–1930	90
Christy Mathewson	1900–1916	79
Cy Young	1890–1911	76
Eddie Plank	1901–1917	69
Warren Spahn	1942–1965	63
Nolan Ryan	1966–1983	61
Tom Seaver	1967–1986	61
Bert Blyleven	1970–1992	60
Don Sutton	1966–1988	58

* **Shutout (ShO or SHO):** when a single pitcher pitches a complete game and does not allow the opposing team to score a run. Totals relate only to a player's MLB career. Between 1919–2011 there were about 120 shutouts in the World Series.

MLB career strikeout* leaders (pitchers)

👤	🔄	⬚
Nolan Ryan	1966–1983	5,714
Randy Johnson	1988–2009	4,875
Roger Clemens	1984–2007	4,672
Steve Carlton	1965–1988	4,136
Bert Blyleven	1970–1992	3,701
Tom Seaver	1967–1986	3,640
Don Sutton	1966–1988	3,574
Gaylord Perry	1962–1983	3,534
Walter Johnson	1907–1927	3,508
Greg Maddux	1986–2008	3,371

* **Strikeout (K or SO):** the number of times a pitcher has caused a batter to make three strikes during the batter's time at bat. Totals relate only to a player's MLB career. The "3,000 strikeout club" (3,000-plus strikeouts) has 16 members to date.

Career MLB wins* leaders

👤	🔄	⬚
Cy Young	1890–1911	511
Walter Johnson	1907–1927	417
Grover Cleveland Alexander	1911–1930	373
Christy Mathewson	1900–1916	373
Pud Galvin	1875–1892	365

* **Wins:** a statistic credited to the pitcher of the winning team who was in the game when his team last took the lead. Totals relate only to a player's MLB career. Only 24 pitchers have amassed 300-plus wins in their career.

Career MLB losses* leaders

👤	🔄	⬚
Cy Young	1890–1911	316
Pud Galvin	1875–1892	308
Nolan Ryan	1966–1983	292
Walter Johnson	1907–1927	279
Phil Niekro	1964–1987	274

* **Loss:** a statistic credited to the pitcher of the losing team who allows the run (the go-ahead run) that gives the opposing team the lead and also eventually the win. Totals relate only to a player's MLB career.

Major League Baseball

MLB

Founded in 1903, MLB is a professional baseball organization of 15 teams from the National League (NL) and 15 teams from the American League (AL). Of the 30 teams, one is from Canada. Each team plays 162 games during the roughly 26-week season. The climax of the season is a best-of-seven-games playoff, the World Series, between the NL and AL champions for the Commissioner's Trophy.

Current teams of MLB

Team based in Toronto, Canada

Current names and locations of all MLB teams.

American League

East division	Central division	West division
Baltimore Orioles	Chicago White Sox	Houston Astros
Boston Red Sox	Cleveland Indians	Los Angeles Angels
New York Yankees	Detroit Tigers	Oakland Athletics
Tampa Bay Rays	Kansas City Royals	Seattle Mariners
Toronto Blue Jays	Minnesota Twins	Texas Rangers

National League

East division	Central division	West division
Atlanta Braves	Chicago Cubs	Arizona Diamondbacks
Miami Marlins	Cincinnati Reds	Colorado Rockies
New York Mets	Milwaukee Brewers	Los Angeles Dodgers
Philadelphia Phillies	Pittsburgh Pirates	San Diego Padres
Washington Nationals	St. Louis Cardinals	San Francisco Giants

World Series team records

	🏆	②	📅★
New York Yankees	27	13	2009
St. Louis Cardinals	11	8	2011
Oakland Athletics	9	5	1989
San Francisco Giants	8	12	2014
Boston Red Sox	8	4	2013
Los Angeles Dodgers	6	13	1988
Cincinnati Reds	5	4	1990
Pittsburgh Pirates	5	2	1979
Detroit Tigers	4	7	1984
Chicago Cubs	3	8	2016
Atlanta Braves	3	6	1995
Baltimore Orioles	3	4	1983
Minnesota Twins	3	3	1991
Chicago White Sox	3	2	2005
Philadelphia Phillies	2	5	2008
Cleveland Indians	2	4	1948
New York Mets	2	3	1986
Kansas City Royals	2	2	2015
Toronto Blue Jays	2	0	1993
Miami Marlins	2	0	2003
Houston Astros	1	1	2017
Arizona Diamondbacks	1	0	2001
Los Angeles Angels	1	0	2002
Texas Rangers	0	2	
San Diego Padres	0	2	
Tampa Bay Rays	0	1	
Colorado Rockies	0	1	
Milwaukee Brewers	0	1	
Washington Nationals	0		
Seattle Mariners	0		

World Series winning streaks (in years)

🏅	📅	📚
New York Yankees*	1949–1953	5
New York Yankees	1936–1939	4
Oakland Athletics	1972–1974	3
New York Yankees	1998–2000	3
Chicago Cubs	1907–1908	2
Philadelphia Athletics	1910–1911	2
Boston Red Sox	1915–1916	2
New York Giants	1921–1922	2
New York Yankees	1927–1928	2
Philadelphia Athletics	1929–1930	2
New York Yankees	1961–1962	2
Cincinnati Reds	1975–1976	2
New York Yankees	1977–1978	2
Toronto Blue Jays	1992–1993	2

* **New York Yankees**: during the period 1947–1964, this team enjoyed a remarkable run, appearing in 15 of the 18 World Series.

Longest World Series droughts (in seasons)

🏅	📅★	📚
Cleveland Indians	1948	69
Texas Rangers	1961*	57
Milwaukee Brewers	1969*	49
San Diego Padres	1969*	49
Washington Nationals	1969*	49
Seattle Mariners	1977*	41
Pittsburgh Pirates	1979	38
Baltimore Orioles	1983	34
Detroit Tigers	1984	33
New York Mets	1986	31
Los Angeles Dodgers	1988	29
Oakland Athletics	1989	28
Cincinnati Reds	1990	27
Minnesota Twins	1991	26
Colorado Rockies	1993*	25

* Team franchise began in the noted year and never won a World Series. For all teams: drought season broken by a World Series win or appearance.

Factfile

🥇 Commissioner's Trophy

This trophy is presented by the Commissioner of Baseball to the winner of the World Series. It was first presented in 1967 to the St. Louis Cardinals, and a new one is made each year. The 24-inch-tall silver trophy features 30 gold-plated flags representing each MLB team.

New York Yankees

The New York Yankees are the most successful MLB postseason team with six winning-streak list entries. During 1949–1953, the likes of Joe DiMaggio, Phil Rizzuto, Mickey Mantle, Vic Raschi and Larry "Yogi" Berra played for the Bronx-based team, winning five World Series.

Nippon Professional Baseball

The Japan Series is the championship of Nippon Professional Baseball. This best-of-seven-games series pits the winners of the Central League and Pacific League against each other. Each league consists of six teams playing 146 regular season games starting in late March. There are two or three All-Star games in July. The winner of the Japan Series represents Japan in the Asia Series.

Japan Series results

	🛡	🏆	②
Yomiuri Giants		22	12
Saitama Seibu Lions		13	8
Fukuoka SoftBank Hawks		8	9
Tokyo Yakult Swallows		5	2
Orix Buffaloes		4	8
Chiba Lotte Marines		4	2
Hiroshima Toyo Carp		3	4
Hokkaido Nippon-Ham Fighters		3	4
Chunichi Dragons		2	8
Yokohama DeNA BayStars		2	1
Hanshin Tigers		1	5
Tohoku Rakuten Golden Eagles		1	0
Osaka Kintetsu Buffaloes*		0	4
Shochiku Robins**		0	1

* Merged with Orix Blue Wave to become Orix Buffaloes.

** Merged with Taiyo Whales and became, after a rename, the Yokohama DeNA BayStars.

Career batting* records

	👤	🚩	📚
Hits			
Isao Harimoto		KOR	3,085
Katsuya Nomura		JPN	2,901
Sadaharu Oh		JPN	2,786
Home runs			
Sadaharu Oh		JPN	868
Katsuya Nomura		JPN	657
Hiromitsu Kadota		JPN	567
Strikeouts			
Kazuhiro Kiyohara		JPN	1,955
Motonobu Tanishige		JPN	1,838
Koji Akiyama		JPN	1,712

* Hits, home runs and strikeouts – *see page 18.*

George Altman

This left-hand batter, right-hand thrower, topped the Pacific League in 1968 for hits (170) and runs (84). He played for Tokyo/Lotte Orions.

Career pitching* records

	👤	🚩	📚
Wins			
Masaichi Kaneda		JAP	400
Tetsuya Yoneda		JAP	350
Masaaki Koyama		JAP	320
Keishi Suzuki		JAP	317
Takehiko Bessho		JAP	310
Victor Starffin		RUS	303
Strikeouts			
Masaichi Kaneda		JAP	4490
Tetsuya Yoneda		JAP	3388
Masaaki Koyama		JAP	3159
Keishi Suzuki		JAP	3061

* Pitching wins and strikeouts – *see page 18.*

Gene Bacque

Bacque was the NPB's first foreign pitcher. He won the Sawamura Award and had a no-hitter in 1965 for the Hanshin Tigers.

Factfile

👤 Sadaharu Oh

Yomiuri Giants' left-handed slugger Oh hit 868 home runs in his career (1959–1980) and made baseball history. In 1978, Oh created the "800 Home Run Club" to mark his 800th home run. Oh is the club's only member. He is known for his "flamingo" leg kick when hitting.

🏆 Fukuoka SoftBank Hawks

The 2017 holders of the Japan Series, the Pacific League Hawks, saw off the Yokohama DeNA BayStars in game 6 to win 4–2. It was their first win since 1998. Dennis Sarfate, the team's US closing pitcher, won the MVP award for his two crucial saves and the win in game 6.

World Baseball Classic

This is an international baseball tournament that occurs every four years and results in the winner being titled World Champion. Some 20 teams have entered the Classic, but only 16 can qualify. The WBC uses multiple hosts spread around the globe, with the championship round held at a US MLB stadium. The first WBC event was in 2005.

WBC team records

🚩	🏆	②
Japan	2	0
Dominican Republic	1	0
USA	1	0
Puerto Rico	0	2
South Korea	0	1
Cuba	0	1

Individual records

	👤	🚩	📚
Home runs			
Alfredo Despaigne		CUB	7
Runs batted in			
Frederich Cepeda		CUB	23
Pitching wins			
Daisuke Matsuzaka		JPN	6
Pitching strikeouts			
Daisuke Matsuzaka		JPN	23

Factfile

👤 Frederich Cepeda

The Cuban outfielder won Olympic baseball gold and silver in 2004 and 2008 with his national team. Cepeda's career high came when he was named in the 2009 All-WBC Classic squad.

⭐ Japan

The Japanese team hoped to add a third WBC win in 2017 to their record sheet. After clear wins in the earlier rounds it looked likely until they lost 2–1 to the US. The US went on to win the WBC.

Australian Baseball League

Founded in 2009, this league consists of six teams who play over the Southern hemisphere summer, often under lights at night. Winners of the annual ABL championships receive the Claxton Shield, named for Norrie Claxton who organized the first national competition. The shield bears the names of Australian baseball champions since 1934.

ABL championship standings

🛡	🏆	②
Perth Heat	4	1
Brisbane Bandits	3	0
Canberra Cavalry	1	2
Melbourne Aces	0	2
Adelaide Bite	0	3

Series MVP* award

👤	📅
Logan Wade	2016–17
Donald Lutz	2015–16
Allan de San Miguel	2014–15
Joey Wong	2013–14
Aaron Sloan	2012–13
Virgil Vasquez	2011–12
Benjamin Moore	2010–11

* **MVP (Most Valuable Player):** this award, voted by the media and online polls, is given to the season's best-performing player/s.

Factfile

👤 Jake Fraley

Winner of the 2017–2018 ABL Most Valuable Player, Fraley plays in Australia for Perth Heat and in his native US for the Tampa Bay Rays. In his first ABL season, he broke the league's stolen base record.

② Adelaide Bite

This South Australian team has made the finals three times but never gone home with the Shield. The team's name alludes to the "bite" of the great white shark and the nearby Great Australian Bight.

Super Teams

St. Louis Cardinals
1942

The '42 team posted the highest winning percentage (.688) in franchise history, lead the league in runs scored and fewest runs allowed, and nailed the Yankees 4–1 in the World Series.

Stan Musial, Enos Slaughter, Mort Cooper.

Atlanta Braves
1995

After losing the World Series in 1991 and 1992, the pressure was on for 1995. And with their overpowering starting pitcher lineup and clutch hitting, a faltering season start ended in glorious victory.

Greg Maddux, Tom Glavine, John Smoltz, Steve Avery.

New York Mets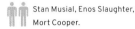
1986

Not the most popular team in MLB, but New Yorkers loved the Mets "bad guys" of '86 who clinched the NL title over the Houston Astros in a nail-biter, and beat the Red Sox to win the World Series.

Jesse Orosco, Mookie Wilson, Bob Ojeda, Ron Darling, Dwight Gooden.

New York Yankees
1927

Known as "Murderer's Row," the feared '27 Yankees lineup is hailed as one of the best ever! They finished with a record 110 victories, won the AL pennant by 19 games, and triumphed in the World Series.

Earle Combs, Mark Koenig, Babe Ruth, Lou Gehrig, Bob Meusel, Tony Lazzeri.

Baltimore Orioles
1970

Things that had been coming together for a few years snapped into place in 1970. The Orioles saw off the New York Yankees and Minnesota Twins, then took the Cincinnati Reds 4–1 in the World Series.

Brooks Robinson, Frank Robinson, Jim Palmer, Boog Powell, Don Buford.

Arizona Diamondbacks
2001

In its fourth season, the D-backs defeated the Yankees for the World Series. No other team has gone from zero to hero so fast! Their strength lay in the one–two pitching partnership of Johnson and Schilling.

Randy Johnson, Curt Schilling, Luis Gonzalez, Miguel Batista.

Cincinnati Reds
1976

The "Big Red Machine" dominated the NL from 1970–1976 and won two World Series. The "Great Eight" of 1975–1976 collected awards and titles by the score, including 26 Gold Gloves and 65 All-Star selections.

Johnny Bench, Tony Pérez, Joe Morgan, Dave Concepción, Pete Rose, Ken Griffey.

Los Angeles Dodgers
1963

The presence of Sandy Koufax alone made the '63 Dodgers a super team. They won the NL by six games over the Cardinals and took the World Series from the favored Yankees in just four games.

Sandy Koufax, Tommy Davis, Don Drysdale, Walter Aston, Maury Wills.

Detroit Tigers
1984

The '84 Tigers had a phenomenal start, winning 87% of their games in the first quarter of this season. They ended the season besting the San Diego Padres in the World Series.

Alan Trammell, Kirk Gibson, Jack Morris, Willie Hernandez.

Oakland Athletics
1972

Suspensions, threats, injuries and missiles from the bleachers colored this team's AL win. In the World Series – "The Hairs v. The Squares" – the longhaired Athletics beat the clean-cut Cincinnati Reds.

Gene Tenace, Reggie Jackson, Rollie Fingers, Catfish Hunter.

A Moment in Time

"The Catch"
New York Giants v. Cleveland Indians

September 29, 1954
Polo Grounds, New York City
World Series Game 1, 8th inning

Willie Mays' over-the-shoulder catch at the warning track is legend. With the score tied, New York Giants' Don Liddle pitched to Cleveland Indians' Vic Wertz. The ball flew to deep center. Mays chased it, grabbed it and gunned it to the infield to hold Cleveland at first and second base with one out!

Controversy

Rubber bat
New York Yankees v. Detroit Tigers

September 7, 1974
Shea Stadium, New York
Regular season MLB series

Drilling out a core section of a bat and filling it with something else is illegal, but no player has been caught cheating like the Yankees' Graig Nettles. He swung his doctored bat for a single, and it broke. Superballs bounced out into the hands of the Tigers' catcher, and Nettles was suspended for 10 days.

Sporting Arenas

Dodger Stadium
This is the third-oldest baseball stadium still in use and has the largest capacity, which can be expanded to seat 85,000. Known as a "pitcher's ballpark," it is home to the Los Angeles Dodgers.

56,000   1962   Los Angeles, California

Fenway Park
The oldest major league stadium, the Red Sox moved in, and then won the 1912 World Series. Its "Green Monster" wall, "The Triangle," "Pesky's Pole" and hand-operated scoreboard are famous.

37,731   1912   Boston, Massachusetts

SunTrust Park
MLB's newest stadium is home to the Atlanta Braves. At its opening, Hank "Hammer" Aaron threw the first pitch. Aaron also threw the last ball at the team's old Turner Field.

41,149   2017   Atlanta, Georgia

BASKETBALL

Modern basketball began as recently as 1891, and quickly became one of the top spectator sports in the world. (Its players are among the highest-paid athletes.) Invented by James W. Naismith, a Canadian sports instructor, the game was designed for playing in a gymnasium indoors, in harsh winters. The first-ever game used a soccer ball and peach baskets (bottoms removed). The sport gained popularity through the YMCA, colleges and schools. There are professional leagues in many countries and countless regional, national, and international competitions. Some 450 million people participate in this fast, exciting and athletic sport.

> "Basketball is a simple game. Your goal is penetration, get the ball close to the basket, and there are three ways to do that: pass, dribble and offensive rebound."
>
> Phil Jones, 11-time NBA championship team coach

All-Stars

Michael "MJ" Jordan

🕐 1984–2003   🏳 USA

With the Chicago Bulls, this phenomenal athlete of power, speed and artistry won six NBA titles, 11 MVP awards and was 14 times an NBA All-Star. His career points of 32,292, rank him fourth on the all-time leader board.

Earvin "Magic" Johnson

🕐 1979–1996   🏳 USA

At 6 ft., 9 in., this Los Angeles Laker point guard used his size to shred defenses. Holder of five NBA titles and three NBA MVP awards, Magic was known for his half-court alley-oop (a pass to a player near the basket who tips it in).

Lauren "Loz" Jackson

🕐 1997–2016   🏳 Australia

This Australian joined the Opals at 16, and three years later was selected by the Seattle Storm. The power forward/center won two WNBA Championships and multiple MVPs, and Olympic and Commonwealth Games medals.

▼ National Basketball Association   [NBA]

The NBA consists of 29 American and one Canadian men's basketball teams. It was founded in 1946. In the regular season, each team plays 82 games (October–April) followed by the championship playoffs. African-Americans first entered the NBA in 1950, and in 1996 the NBA created the Women's National Basketball League (WNBA).

Current teams of the NBA

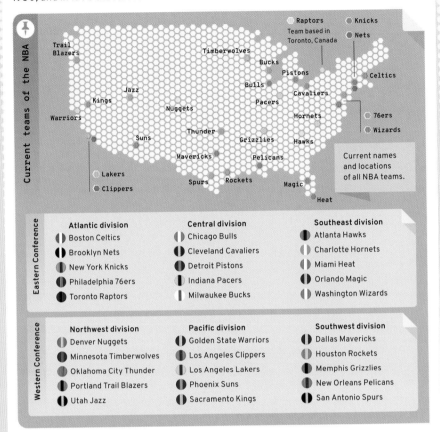

Current names and locations of all NBA teams.

Eastern Conference

Atlantic division
- Boston Celtics
- Brooklyn Nets
- New York Knicks
- Philadelphia 76ers
- Toronto Raptors

Central division
- Chicago Bulls
- Cleveland Cavaliers
- Detroit Pistons
- Indiana Pacers
- Milwaukee Bucks

Southeast division
- Atlanta Hawks
- Charlotte Hornets
- Miami Heat
- Orlando Magic
- Washington Wizards

Western Conference

Northwest division
- Denver Nuggets
- Minnesota Timberwolves
- Oklahoma City Thunder
- Portland Trail Blazers
- Utah Jazz

Pacific division
- Golden State Warriors
- Los Angeles Clippers
- Los Angeles Lakers
- Phoenix Suns
- Sacramento Kings

Southwest division
- Dallas Mavericks
- Houston Rockets
- Memphis Grizzlies
- New Orleans Pelicans
- San Antonio Spurs

NBA champions, by wins

⭐	🏆	②	📅⭐
Boston Celtics*	17	4	2008
Los Angeles Lakers*	16	15	2010
Golden State Warriors	6	4	2018
Chicago Bulls	6	0	1998
San Antonio Spurs	5	1	2014
Philadelphia 76ers	3	6	1983
Detroit Pistons	3	4	2004
Miami Heat	3	2	2013
New York Knicks	2	6	1973
Houston Rockets	2	2	1995
Cleveland Cavaliers	1	4	2016
Atlanta Hawks	1	3	1958
Washington Wizards	1	3	1978
Oklahoma City Thunder	1	3	1979
Portland Trail Blazers	1	2	1977
Milwaukee Bucks	1	1	1971
Dallas Mavericks	1	1	2011
Sacramento Kings	1	0	1951

* These two teams have an intense rivalry, and they have faced each other a record 12 times in the NBA Finals.

Factfile

🏆 **Golden State Warriors**

NBA finals champions for 2018, the Oakland-based Warriors defeated the Cleveland Cavaliers 4–0 – the first clean sweep in the NBA since 2007. It was the fourth year in a row that these two faced each other in the finals.

👤 **Wilt Chamberlain**

Only once in NBA history has a player scored 100 points in a single game. Wilt Chamberlain, center for the then-Philadelphia Warriors (now the Golden State Warriors), set this record on March 2, 1962, against the New York Knicks at the Hershey Arena in Pennsylvania.

EuroLeague Basketball

FIBA Europe organizes professional indoor basketball competitions among European (plus Israel) clubs. Founded under a different name in 1957, there are currently 16 clubs, each playing up to 37 games in the regular season. Playoffs for the championship Final Four and the EuroLeague Trophy follow.

Multiple titles

🛡	🏳	🏆	❷
Real Madrid	ESP	10	8
CSKA Moscow	RUS	7	6
Maccabi Tel Aviv	ISR	6	9
Panathinaikos	GRC	6	1
Varese	ITA	5	5
Olympiacos	GRC	3	5
Olimpia Milano	ITA	3	2
Rīgas ASK	URS	3	1
Split	YUG	3	1
FC Barcelona	ESP	2	5
Virtus Bologna	ITA	2	3
Cantù	ITA	2	0
Cibona	YUG	2	0

At the 2012 final, Olympiacos made up a 19-point deficit against CSKA Moscow. They sealed the deal with a field goal seconds before the buzzer!

Factfile

Real Madrid

This team is as successful as the well-known soccer team Real Madrid C.F. They are 2018 EuroLeague champions and hold 33 Spanish League championships plus multiple Intercontinental Cup titles.

Alphonso Ford

Though this American shooting guard was also in the NBA, it was in the EuroLeague that he made his name. He was one of the league's greatest-ever scorers. He died of leukemia at just 32.

Focus on the Olympics

Men's basketball officially started at the Berlin games in 1936; the women's game in 1976. The 1936 final – USA v. Canada – was held on a muddy clay tennis court outdoors (the first and last time) in the rain. The heavy lopsided ball made dribbling impossible. Olympic basketball has come a long way since, but Team USA continue to win!

Olympic medal leaders, by gold

🏳	●	●	●	○
Men				
USA	15	1	2	18
URS*	2	4	3	9
YUG	1	4	1	6
ARG	1	0	1	2
Women				
USA	8	1	1	10
URS*	2	0	1	3
EUN	1	0	0	1

* The success of Soviet Union (URS) teams to 1991 has not been equaled by Russian (RUS) teams.

All-time top points scorers

👤	🏳	🏀
Men		
Oscar Schmidt	BRA	1,093
Women		
Lauren Jackson	AUS	575

Factfile

"Dream Team"

This 1992 US Olympic team included Magic Johnson, Michael Jordan, Larry Bird and Patrick Ewing. The team scored more than 100 points per game on their way to the gold medal.

Olympic final 1972
USA v. Soviet Union

America has always disputed its 50–51 loss against Cold War enemy, the Soviet Union. The Americans claim they won 50–49, but three seconds "extra" play allowed the Soviets to score.

Sporting Arenas

Philippine Arena

This is the world's largest indoor arena with seating arranged in a semicircle around the action. In addition to hosting basketball and other sports, it is a venue for its owners, the Church of Christ.

👥 55,000   🔧 2014   📍 Bulacan, Philippines

Madison Square Garden

This multi-purpose venue, known as "The Garden," is home to the New York Knicks (NBA) and the Liberty (WNBA) and hosts Big East Conference and National Invitation Tournaments.

👥 20,789   🔧 1968   📍 New York, New York

Cameron Indoor Stadium

A mecca for American college basketball, this arena is part of Duke University. It is known for the volume of its fans' chanting. Chants can reach 123.1 decibels (a power saw at three feet).

👥 9,314   🔧 1940   📍 Durham, North Carolina

Wheelchair Basketball

This is a fast and furious game where aluminum and titanium collide. It mirrors the running version except that a player's feet may not touch the floor or be used to steer. A violation occurs if there are more than two wheel pushes in possession without dribbling. Hoop height remains the same, meaning that scoring from the low-seated wheelchair is even more impressive.

Paralympic medal leaders, by gold

🏳	●	●	●	○
Men				
USA	8	1	4	13
Canada	3	1	0	4
Israel	2	2	3	7
Australia	2	2	0	4
Netherlands	1	5	0	6
France	1	0	3	4
Women				
USA	4	1	3	8
Germany	3	4	0	7
Canada	3	0	1	4
Israel	2	2	1	5
Argentina	1	1	1	3

Individual Paralympic medalists

👤	🏳	●	●	●	○
Patrick Anderson	CAN	3	1	0	4
Tracey Ferguson	CAN	3	0	1	4

Superstar ⭐

Patrick Anderson

Regarded as the best wheelchair basketball player in the world, Anderson lost both legs below the knee when he was nine. He competed with the Canadian team in four Paralympics, winning three gold medals. Now living in the US, he plays with the New York Rollin' Knicks.

🔄 1997–   🏳 Canada

Para Athletes

BOXING

Boxing is as old as humankind. It is depicted in art dating back 5,000 years. The ancient Greeks developed it into a sport. The boxers' hands were bound in leather straps and the ring was a chalked circle. The 1867 rules of modern boxing – the Queensbury rules – specified gloves and ring size, duration of matches, and the 10-second count for a knockout. While professional boxers fight for money, only amateurs may compete in the Olympic and Commonwealth Games. Amateur boxers wear headgear, weight-specified gloves and fight fewer rounds than professionals. Though boxing rules aim to ensure a clean, fair and safe fight, head injuries are common.

> "The fight is won or lost far away from witnesses – behind the lines, in the gym and out there on the road, long before I dance under those lights."
>
> Muhammad Ali, three-time heavyweight boxing champion

All-Stars

Muhammad Ali

1960–1981   USA

Known as "The Greatest," this heavyweight was a showman, activist and celebrated sportsperson. His fights, like "Thrilla in Manilla," and "The Rumble in the Jungle" are legend. Ali had 61 bouts; he won 56 (including 37 knockouts).

"Sugar Ray" Robinson

1940–1965   USA

Robinson was a world welterweight and middleweight champion. Known as the greatest "pound for pound" boxer, he could throw every standard punch equally powerfully with both hands and land a knockout blow going backward.

Rocco "Rocky" Marciano

1947–1956   USA

Nicknamed the "The Brockton Blockbuster," he is the only heavyweight champion to retire undefeated. He won all of his 49 bouts, including 43 by knockout. He fought in a crouch, laying relentless, powerful punches.

Record Breakers

Undefeated boxing World Champions

Jimmy Barry	USA	59-0-9	1894–1899
Ricardo López	MEX	51-0-1	1990–2002
Floyd Mayweather Jr.	USA	50-0-0	1998–2017
Rocky Marciano	USA	49-0-0	1952–1956
Joe Calzaghe	GBR	46-0-0	1997–2008
Sven Ottke	GER	34-0-0	1998–2004
Andre Ward	USA	32-0-0	2009–2017
Jack McAuliffe	USA	30-0-5	1886–1893
Harry Simon	NAM	30-0-0	1998–2002
Mihai Leu	ROM	28-0-0	1997
Edwin Valero	VEN	27-0-0	2006–2010
Terry Marsh	GBR	26-0-1	1987
Pichit Sitbangprachan	THA	24-0-0	1992–1994
Dmitry Pirog	RUS	20-0-0	2010–2012
Kim Ji-won	KOR	16-0-2	1985–1986

Record: the numbers represent, in order, matches won, lost and tied.

The "iron men" of boxing

Willie Pepe	USA	230-11-1
Archie Moore	USA	183-24-10
Sugar Ray Robinson	USA	175-19-6
Ted "Kid" Lewis	GBR	173-30-14
Sam Langford	CAN	167-38-37
Henry Armstrong	USA	151-21-9
Sandy Saddler	USA	144-16-2
Tony Canzoneri	USA	137-24-10
Julio César Chávez	MEX	108-6-2
Marcel Cerdan	ALG	106-4-0

Record: the numbers represent, in order, matches won, lost and tied.

Most fights in one year

Ted "Kid" Lewis	GBR	1911	58
Len Wickwar	GBR	1934	58
Joe Grim	ITA	1902	53
Len Wickwar	GBR	1935	51
Len Wickwar	GBR	1932	50
Len Wickwar	GBR	1933	49
Len Wickwar	GBR	1936	48
John "Unk" Russell	USA	1905	46
Len Wickwar	GBR	1930	44
Harry Greb	USA	1919	44

Most wins by knockout*

Billy Bird	GBR	138
Archie Moore	USA	132
Young Stribling	USA	129
Sam Langford	CAN	128
Buck Smith	USA	120
Luis "Kid Azteca" Paramo	MEX	114
George Odwell	GBR	111
"Sugar Ray" Robinson	USA	108
"Alabama Kid" Reeves	USA	108
Peter Maher	IRL	107
Sandy Saddler	USA	103

* Knockout (KO): when one boxer is unable to rise from the canvas within a count of 10, the other is declared the winner.

Oldest world champions

Bernard Hopkins	USA	48
George Foreman	USA	45
"Sugar Boy" Malinga	RSA	41
Bob Fitzsimmons	GBR	40
Roberto Durán	PAN	37
Joe Walcott	USA	37
Evander Holyfield	USA	37
Corrie Sanders	RSA	37
Daniel Zaragoza	MEX	37
Azumah Nelson	GHA	37
Muhammad Ali	USA	36

Longest reigning heavyweights* (in days)

Wladimir Klitschko	UKR	4,382
Joe Louis	USA	4,270
Muhammad Ali	USA	3,443
Lennox Lewis	GBR	3,086
Vitali Klitschko	UKR	2,735
Larry Holmes	USA	2,661
Jack Dempsey	USA	2,638
John Sullivan	USA	2,566
Jack Johnson	USA	2,292
Evander Holyfield	USA	2,223

* Heavyweight: a weight class for boxers weighing over 200 lb. It is the premier class in professional boxing.

Biggest grossing* fights

Floyd Mayweather Jr. v. Conor McGregor	
2017	$500 million
Floyd Mayweather Jr. v. Manny Pacquiao	
2015	$410 million
Floyd Mayweather Jr. v. Saúl "Canelo" Álvarez	
2013	$150 million

* Grossing: all monies (revenue) taken in by the fight promoter. The boxers are paid from this purse.

Boxing   Combat sports

COMBAT SPORTS

Martial arts started 6,000 years ago in China. There are 148 types of martial arts. In a match, two fighters aim to defeat each other outright, or to win on points. Taekwondo developed from karate and Chinese and Korean martial arts. Its head-high kicks, jumps and spin kicks require speed and agility. Judo, meaning "yielding way," is based on jujitsu styles and employs throwing and ground grappling moves. Mixed Martial Arts (MMA) allows kicking, punching and grappling techniques from boxing, karate, jujitsu, wrestling and judo. Combat sport competitions are categorized into weight classes. MMA is not yet an Olympic or Paralympic event.

> "A real strong fighter should always look dignified and calm, and I believe that any expression of aggression is an expression of weakness."
>
> Fedor Emelianenko, heavyweight MMA champion

All-Stars

Fedor Emelianenko

 2000–   Russia

This Ukrainian-born Russian MMA heavyweight is acclaimed for his multiple championship wins and eight-year run as No. 1 heavyweight MMA. "The Last Emperor" is known for his total mastery, footwork and signature Russian hook.

Yasuhiro Yamashita

 1976–1985   Japan

This sixth-degree black belt judo artist had a winning streak of 203 matches. He was the youngest-ever All-Japan Champion and won that title eight further times, along with five world titles, including Olympic gold.

Hadi Saei

 1995–2008   Iran

The determination and strength of this Iranian taekwondo athlete were on display in his 2008 Olympic final. He won the bout with a broken hand! Hadi held nine international titles and his win rate was a staggering 90%.

Ultimate Fighting Championship   `UFC`

This is the world's largest MMA promotion organization and it has hosted some 400 events. During the 1990s, the rules were changed to remove "no holds barred" fighting and UFC came to be seen as a sport. Since 2012 there has also been a women's MMA event. Fights are held in an eight-sided cage (The Octagon), and bouts last for no more than five minutes, with a maximum of five bouts. There are nine weight classes.

Longest individual UFC reigns (in days)

🏃	🚩	📚
Anderson Silva	BRA	2,457
Demetrious Johnson	USA	2,142
Georges St-Pierre	CAN	2,064
José Aldo	BRA	1,848
Jon Jones	USA	1,501
Tito Ortiz	USA	1,260
Daniel Cormier	USA	1,183
Dominick Cruz	USA	1,117
Ronda Rousey	USA	1,074
Joanna Jedrzejczyk	POL	966

Most championship title wins

🏆	📈	📚
Georges St-Pierre	13–2–0	13
Demetrious Johnson	12–1–0	12
Anderson Silva*	11–2–0	11
Jon Jones	10–0–0	10

*Silva's 16 consecutive victories (2006–2013) is also a record.

Factfile

 Ronda Rousey

Ronda Rousey was the first female UFC champion, defending her 135-pound bantamweight title for over three years. She was the first American to win Olympic bronze in judo (2008), and the first female fighter in the UFC Hall of Fame.

 Anytime, any weight, anywhere
Conor McGregor v. Nate Diaz

In March 2016, the UFC champ McGregor shared the cage with upstart Diaz. By round two McGregor was bleeding in a Diaz clinch. Diaz's short punches, straight left followed by a guillotine and choke left the champ tapping out submission.

Focus on the Olympics

Wrestling was part of the Olympics in 648 BCE, but boxing (see page 24), fencing, judo and taekwondo are 20th-century additions. In foil, épée and sabre fencing, points are scored when the weapon's electronic tip makes contact with the opponent's jacketed torso. The aim in judo is to immobilize or ground the opponent. In Olympic sparring taekwondo, the two combatants score points for each full-contact kick.

Top gold-medal athletes, by sport

🏃	🚩	🥇	🥈	🥉	⭕
Boxing					
László Papp	HUN	3	0	0	3
Félix Savón	CUB	3	0	0	3
Teófilo Stevenson	CUB	3	0	0	3
Fencing					
Aladár Gerevich	HUN	7	1	2	10
Judo					
Tadahiro Nomura	JPN	3	0	0	3
Taekwondo					
Hwang Kyung-seon	KOR	2	0	1	3
Steven López	USA	2	0	1	3
Hadi Saei	IRI	2	0	1	3
Chen Zhong	CHN	2	0	0	2
Jade Jones	GBR	2	0	0	2
Wu Jingyu	CHN	2	0	0	2
Wrestling					
Kaori Icho	JPN	4	0	0	4

Factfile

 Aladár Gerevich

This Hungarian fencer competed in six Olympics between 1932 and 1960 and won the sabre team event six times – a unique record! To compete in the 1960 games at age 50, he proved himself by challenging the sabre team and winning every match.

 Kaori Icho

Icho dominated freestyle wrestling from 2003–2016 in the middle- and welterweight divisions. Her winning streak covered 189 matches. She was world champion 10 times and in four Olympics won four gold medals for Japan.

MOTORSPORTS

What started with a city-to-city road race in France in 1894 has grown into a multi-billion-dollar global sport with millions of fans. Within four-wheeled racing there are open-wheel car races (F1 and IndyCar) and closed-wheel car races (rallying and Daytona). In two-wheeled motorbike (or moto) racing, the premier events are Grand Prix, superbike and road racing, such as the Isle of Man TT. Motorsports – car and motorbike – use purpose-built circuits, or temporarily closed street circuits. Professional drivers and riders, backed by expert teams, aim to get their vehicle safely to the checkered flag first, completing the required number of laps in the fastest time.

> "When I was very young, I busted my nose when I was racing. The first thing my dad asked me was: 'Are you OK?' I said, 'Can you fix the car for tomorrow?'"
>
> Lewis Hamilton, F1 champion (2008, 2014, 2015, 2017)

All-Stars

Michael Schumacher
🕐 1991–2012   🏁 Germany

This German driver known for his pace and tactical genius holds records for the most F1 championships (seven), Grand Prix wins (91), fastest laps (77) and wins in a season (13). In 2013, he suffered a brain injury in a skiing accident.

Alain Prost
🕐 1980–1993   🏁 France

Frenchman Prost won 51 races and was on the podium 106 times in 199 F1 starts. Nicknamed "The Professor" because of his analytical approach to competition and car setup, he and Brazilian Ayrton Senna were fierce rivals.

Juan Manuel Fangio
🕐 1950–1958   🏁 Argentina

This Argentinian driver, "The Master," dominated F1's early years. His fifth championship came at the German Grand Prix in 1957, where he broke – and rebroke – lap speed records nine times to make up for a slow pit stop.

▼ Formula One   FIA

The first F1 drivers' championship was in 1950, with the constructors' (those that own the design of an F1 car) championship eight years later. The FIA determines the cars' technical specifications and race rules. There are currently 21 races in a season, held on circuits around the world. The 305-km race uses a starting grid, with the fastest qualifying car in pole position. During the two-hour race, speeds can exceed 200 kph.

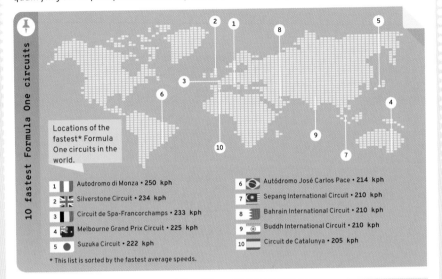

10 fastest Formula One circuits

Locations of the fastest* Formula One circuits in the world.

1 Autodromo di Monza • 250 kph
2 Silverstone Circuit • 234 kph
3 Circuit de Spa-Francorchamps • 233 kph
4 Melbourne Grand Prix Circuit • 225 kph
5 Suzuka Circuit • 222 kph
6 Autódromo José Carlos Pace • 214 kph
7 Sepang International Circuit • 210 kph
8 Bahrain International Circuit • 210 kph
9 Buddh International Circuit • 210 kph
10 Circuit de Catalunya • 205 kph

* This list is sorted by the fastest average speeds.

Multiple F1 driver champions

👤	🏁	🏆
Michael Schumacher	GER	7
Juan Manuel Fangio	ARG	5
Alain Prost	FRA	4
Lewis Hamilton	GBR	4
Sebastian Vettel	GER	4
Jack Brabham	AUS	3
Jackie Stewart	GBR	3
Niki Lauda	AUT	3
Nelson Piquet	BRA	3
Ayrton Senna	BRA	3
Alberto Ascari	ITA	2
Graham Hill	GBR	2
Jim Clark	GBR	2
Emerson Fittipaldi	BRA	2
Mika Häkkinen	FIN	2
Fernando Alonso	ESP	2

F1 constructor champions

🛡	🏁	🏆
Ferrari	ITA	16
Williams	GBR	9
McLaren	GBR	8
Lotus*	GBR	7
Red Bull	AUT	4
Mercedes	GER	4
Cooper*	GBR	2
Brabham*	GBR	2
Renault	FRA	2
Vanwall*	GBR	1
BRM*	GBR	1
Matra*	FRA	1
Tyrrell*	GBR	1
Benetton*	GBR	1
Brawn*	GBR	1

* Contructor teams no longer competing in F1.

| Factfile

👤 Ayrton Senna

On May 1, 1994, during the San Marino Grand Prix, three-time F1 champion Senna was killed when his car hit a barrier at 135 mph. Still considered to be F1's all-time greatest driver, his death was mourned around the world and prompted improved safety rules.

The Monaco duel
Nigel Mansell v. Ayrton Senna

The rivalry between these British and Brazilian drivers was strong, coming to blows in 1987, and wheel-to-wheel, sparks-flying racing in 1991. At the 1992 Grand Prix, they dueled for the final three laps, with Mansell unable to pass Senna, who finished 0.2 seconds ahead.

IndyCar Series

The IndyCar Series currently consists of 17 races on American speedway, road and street circuits. The premier race is the Indianapolis 500. The "500" represents the race length – 500 miles. Teams may only use the chassis and engines prescribed by IndyCar. Top speeds on the tracks are 205–220 mph, except on the Indy 500 speedway where they top out at 235–240 mph. The series winner receives the Astor Cup.

Championship wins by drivers

		🏆
Dario Franchitti	GBR	4
Scott Dixon	NZL	4
Sam Hornish Jr.	USA	3

Course discipline* trophies

A.J. Foyt Trophy (track circuits)

		🏆
Juan Pablo Montoya	COL	2
Hélio Castroneves	BRA	2

Mario Andretti Trophy (road circuits)

		🏆
Will Power	AUS	5

* Disciplines: trophies are awarded to track course and road/street course champions.

Championship wins by teams

	🏆
Chip Ganassi Racing	7
Andretti Autosport	4
Team Penske	4

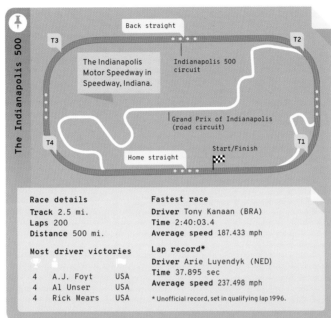

The Indianapolis 500

Back straight

T3   T2

The Indianapolis Motor Speedway in Speedway, Indiana.

Indianapolis 500 circuit

Grand Prix of Indianapolis (road circuit)

T4   T1

Home straight   Start/Finish

Race details
Track 2.5 mi.
Laps 200
Distance 500 mi.

Most driver victories

🏆		
4	A.J. Foyt	USA
4	Al Unser	USA
4	Rick Mears	USA

Fastest race
Driver Tony Kanaan (BRA)
Time 2:40:03.4
Average speed 187.433 mph

Lap record*
Driver Arie Luyendyk (NED)
Time 37.895 sec
Average speed 237.498 mph

* Unofficial record, set in qualifying lap 1996.

Factfile

Dario Franchitti

British driver Franchitti competed in 151 IndyCar Series races during his 11-year career (2002–2013), collecting 21 wins, 57 podium finishes and four IndyCar championships. His driving career ended after a crash at the Grand Prix of Houston.

Chip Ganassi Racing

When this open-wheel racing team won their class at the 2018 Rolex 24 At Daytona, it marked their 200th win. In 2011, Ganassi had the Grand Slam – season wins in the Daytona and Indianapolis 500s, Brickyard 400, and Rolex 24 At Daytona.

NASCAR Cup Series

This US-based series has 36 races, culminating in a champion driver and manufacturer. Points are accumulated on the basis of finishing place and number of laps in the lead. The cars can hit speeds of over 200 mph. Their chassis and bodies are regulated, but their weight and stripped-back aerodynamics mean handling suffers. The Cup Series is raced on 23 tracks across the US.

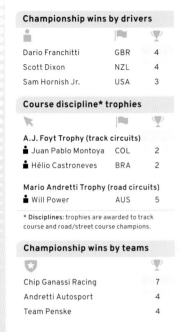

10 fastest modern NASCAR racetracks

Circuits with fastest qualifying speed since 2000.

Chicagoland   Michigan

Home of the Indianapolis Motor Speedway

Kansas   Indiana

Las Vegas   Talladega   Charlotte

Auto Club   Atlanta

Texas   Daytona

1 Michigan Speedway **203.241 mph**
2 Daytona International Speedway **196.434 mph**
3 Texas Motor Speedway **196.235 mph**
4 Atlanta Motor Speedway **194.690 mph**
5 Charlotte Motor Speedway **193.216 mph**
6 Talladega Superspeedway **191.712 mph**
7 Kansas Speedway **191.360 mph**
8 Las Vegas Motor Speedway **190.456 mph**
9 Auto Club Speedway **188.245 mph**
10 Chicagoland Speedway **188.147 mph**

Series* champions, by driver

		🏆
Richard Petty	USA	7
Dale Earnhardt	USA	7
Jimmie Johnson	USA	7
Jeff Gordon	USA	4
Lee Petty	USA	3
David Pearson	USA	3
Cale Yarborough	USA	3
Darrell Waltrip	USA	3
Tony Stewart	USA	3

Series* wins by manufacturer

	🏆
Chevrolet	39
Ford	15
Hudson	3
Toyota	2
Dodge	2
Buick	2

* These lists cover from 1949–2017.

Factfile

Richard Petty

Petty's racing career spanned 35 years (1958–1992) and 1,184 races. "The King" won seven NASCAR championships, and was a seven-time Daytona 500 winner – in total this highly respected driver won 200 races and had over 700 top-10 finishes.

Danica Patrick

Patrick's interest in racing started when she was just ten years old. She went on to set many records for women drivers, including the most top-10 finishes. Patrick was the first woman to get a top-five Indy 500 finish, and to be in pole in a NASCAR Cup Series. Her last race before retiring was the 2018 Daytona.

24 Hours of Le Mans FIA

This epic race, held on the 13.6-km public road and circuit track at Sarthe, France, is the premier event in endurance racing. The race runs continually for 24 hours; constructer teams can cover over 5,000 km. The teams consist of three drivers taking two four-hour shifts at the wheel. The aim is to make it to the end without a mechanical failure or race incident. In 2018, 60 cars started, but only 41 finished Le Mans.

Most wins by driver

Tom Kristensen	DEN	9
Jacky Ickx	BEL	6
Derek Bell	GBR	5
Frank Biela	GER	5
Emanuele Pirro	ITA	5
Olivier Gendebien	BEL	4
Henri Pescarolo	FRA	4
Yannick Dalmas	FRA	4

Consecutive wins by driver

Tom Kristensen	DEN	6
Woolf Barnato	GBR	3
Olivier Gendebien	BEL	3
Henri Pescarolo	FRA	3
Jacky Ickx	BEL	3
Emanuele Pirro	ITA	3
Frank Biela	GER	3
Marco Werner	GER	3

Multiple wins by constructor

Porsche	GER	19
Audi	GER	13
Ferrari	ITA	9
Jaguar	GBR	7
Bentley	GBR	6
Alfa Romeo	ITA	4
Ford	USA	4
Matra-Simca	FRA	3
Peugeot	FRA	3
Lorraine-Dietrich	FRA	2
Bugatti	FRA	2

Consecutive wins by constructor

		📅
Porsche*	7	1981–1987
Ferrari	6	1960–1965
Audi	5	2004–2008
Audi	5	2010–2014

* Winning cars were Porsche 956, 936 and 962C.

Triple Crown* winners

		●	●	●
Hurley Haywood	USA	5	2	3
Andy Wallace	GBR	3	2	1
Al Holbert	USA	2	2	3
A.J. Foyt	USA	2	1	1
Mauro Baldi	ITA	2	1	1
Marco Werner	GER	1	3	3
Jacky Ickx	BEL	1	2	6
Phil Hill	USA	1	2	3
Hans Herrmann	GER	1	2	1
Timo Bernhard	GER	1	1	2
Dan Gurney	USA	1	1	1
Jackie Oliver	GBR	1	1	1

● Rolex 24 At Daytona
● 12 Hours of Sebring
● 24 Hours of Le Mans

* In automobile endurance racing, three events form the Triple Crown. They are considered three of the most challenging endurance races: Rolex 24 at Daytona, 12 Hours of Sebring, and 24 Hours of Le Mans.

Factfile

Porsche

This German car manufacturer has entered over 800 Porsches in Le Mans since 1951. Its first win came the same year; its second not until 1970, but it has dominated since. The 1970 race was a Porsche and Ferrari "Battle of the Titans" – the greatest-ever race.

Tom Kristensen

"Mister Le Mans" is the most successful driver at Le Mans. Of his nine wins, six were consecutive (2000–2005). This Dane drove Audis, Bentleys, BMWs and Porsches. Kristensen also holds the record for six 12 Hours of Sebring wins. He retired in 2014.

World Rally Championship FIA

The first championship was held in 1973, and currently is raced with World Rally Car (WRC) spec'd 1.6-liter, four-cylinder production cars with lots of enhancements. There are 13 three-day rallies broken into 15–30 stages on gravel, tarmac, dirt, snow and ice. There are both driver and constructor titles. A rally car can cost over $600,000.

Multiple titles by drivers

Sébastien Loeb	FRA	9
Sébastien Ogier	FRA	5
Juha Kankkunen	FIN	4
Tommi Mäkinen	FIN	4
Walter Röhrl	GER	2
Miki Biasion	ITA	2
Carlos Sainz	ESP	2
Marcus Grönholm	FIN	2

Multiple titles by constructor

Lancia	ITA	10
Citroën	FRA	8
Peugeot	FRA	5
Volkswagen	GER	4
Fiat	ITA	3
Subaru	JPN	3
Toyota	JPN	3
Audi	GER	3

Factfile

Sébastien Loeb

Nicknamed "The Boss" for his skill on tarmac, Loeb is rallying's most successful competitor. He retired in 2013 after nine consecutive drivers' titles and 78 wins. He came back to racing in 2018.

Lancia

The Italian manufacturer Lancia (Fiat SpA) had 10 wins from 1973 to 1992. Its victories came with the Stratos and 037 models, and with the Delta model with Miki Biasion at the wheel. Lancia stopped rallying in 1992.

World Touring Car Championship FIA

Known as "tin tops," these cars look like the same models you see on the road, but underneath they conform to the FIA's regulations and are heavily modified. Touring car events (2005–2017) were held on purpose-built or closed road circuits around the world. In 2018, the championship became known as the World Touring Car Cup (WTCR).

Multiple titles by drivers*

Yvan Muller	FRA	4
Andy Priaulx	GBR	3
José María López	ARG	3
Gabriele Tarquini	ITA	1
Robert Huff	GBR	1
Thed Björk	SWE	1

Multiple titles by manufacturer*

BMW	GER	3
Chevrolet	USA	3
Citroën	FRA	3
SEAT	ESP	2
Honda	JPN	1
Volvo	SWE	1

* These lists cover 1987–2017. The 2017 WTCC driver's champion was Thed Björk (Polestar Cyan Racing) driving a Volvo S60 Polestar TC1. Volvo won the manufacturers' championship.

Factfile

Yvan Muller

This Frenchman has competed in many motorsports, but found success in touring cars. He has driven for SEAT, Chevrolet and Citroën teams. He is currently racing in a self-owned Hyundai.

Chevrolet

Chevrolet entered the WTCC in 2005, and after three constructor titles, left the series in 2012. It enjoyed 55 wins with a 2.0-liter naturally aspirated and a 1.6-liter turbocharged Chevrolet Cruze.

Grand Prix Motorcycle Racing

This is the oldest motorsport race in the world. It is divided into three classes: MotoGP (1,000 cc maximum), Moto2 (600 cc) and Moto3 (250 cc). The bikes are not production models, but purpose built for racing and not street legal. Currently there are 19 races in the Grand Prix season, and they are held on circuits in 16 countries.

MotoGP titles, by rider

		🏆
Giacomo Agostini	ITA	8
Valentino Rossi	ITA	7
Mick Doohan	AUS	5
Geoff Duke	GBR	4
John Surtees	GBR	4
Mike Hailwood	GBR	4
Eddie Lawson	USA	4
Marc Márquez*	ESP	4

MotoGP titles, by constructor

		🏆
Honda	JPN	19
MV Agusta	ITA	18
Yamaha	JPN	17
Suzuki	JPN	6
Gilera	ITA	6

* Marc Márquez set a MotoGP record of 217.79 mph in 2015, but finished fifth in the race!

Factfile

 Valentino Rossi

Rossi took Honda, Yamaha, Ducati and Aprilia to nine championship wins during MotoGP's most competitive era. His bravery and ability mean he can ride any surface in any condition.

 Marc Márquez

This Spanish rider earned his fourth MotoGP win in 2017. Only Márquez, Mike Hailwood, Phil Read and Valentino Rossi have won championships in all three Grand Prix classes.

Superbike World Championship

Racers in this series ride tuned versions of production bikes that are available to the public. There are currently eight manufacturers and 23 teams competing in Superbike. All bikes use the tires specified by the sport's governing body, FIM. The series, held on permanent circuits around the world, consists of 13 rounds of two races.

Multiple titles by rider

		🏆
Carl Fogarty	GBR	4
Troy Bayliss	AUS	3
Jonathan Rea	GBR	3
Fred Merkel	GBR	2
Doug Polen	USA	2
Colin Edwards	USA	2
Troy Corser	AUS	2
James Toseland	GBR	2
Max Biaggi	ITA	2

Multiple titles by constructor

		🏆
Ducati	ITA	17
Honda	JPN	4
Aprilia	ITA	4
Kawasaki	JPN	3
Suzuki	JPN	1
Yamaha	JPN	1

Factfile

 Carl "Foggy" Fogarty

The most successful Superbike racer ever, this British rider was known for taking the corners at unbelievable speeds. In 219 Superbike starts, he recorded 59 wins and 48 fastest laps.

 Ducati

This famous Italian marque won its first championship in 1990, and success continued with riders Carl Fogarty, Troy Corser and Troy Bayliss. The Ducati 916 won four Superbike championships.

Bandit Big Rig Series

After a gap of some years, rig racing on short tracks (0.5 mi.) is thriving again in the US. Weighing a minimum of 12,000 lb., and with engines and chassis regulated, the big semi-trucks race (and crash) at speeds up to 99 mph. There are 18 events of 8–12 laps, fought by 11 teams and 20 trucks from a rolling start.

2017 top 15 final standings*

1	Ricky Proffitt	4691.5
2	Tommy Boileau	4679.5
3	Justin Ball	4554.5
	Mike Morgan	4554.5
4	Allen Boles	4199.0
5	Chris Kikelhan	3776.5
6	Darren Proffitt	3548.0
7	Jonathan Lisenbee	3497.5
8	Travis Buckner	3437.0
9	Scott Treadway	3198.0
10	Tyler Kruckeberg	3090.5
11	Craig Kruckeberg	2998.5
12	Trevor Kruckeberg	1946.5
13	Robbie Decker	1495.0
14	Joey Seaman	1658.5
15	Cody Slowinski	1245.5

* Big Rig racing does not distinguish between professional and amateur drivers/teams.

Factfile

 Ricky "Rude" Proffitt

Big Rig champion of 2017, Proffitt races for his Rude Motorsports team. A trucker for 20 years, he almost gave away his 192-point lead when he lost ninth gear in the last race.

 Kruckeberg Motorsports

One of the most successful Big Rig outfits, the four-man team race Ford, Kenworth, Peterbilt and Volvo 10-speed trucks. In 2017, team head Craig Kruckeberg won the Hard Charger award.

F1 Powerboat World Championship

The six-meter-long, single-seat Kevlar and carbon fiber boats are not only fast (up to 136 mph) but highly maneuverable on the 350-meter-long course with its multiple turns. At maximum speed, only an inch of hull is in the water; the rest is almost airborne! The championship started in 1981, and races are held around the world.

Title winners by drivers

		🏆
Guido Cappellini	ITA	10
Alex Carella	ITA	4
Scott Gillman	USA	4
Philippe Chiappe	FRA	3
Renato Molinari	ITA	3
Sami Seliö	FIN	2
Jonathan Jones	GBR	2
Jay Price	USA	1
Fabrizio Bocca	ITA	1
John Hill	GBR	1
Gene Thibodaux	USA	1
Bob Spalding	GBR	1
Roger Jenkins	GBR	1

A Super License is required to drive an F1 boat. Drivers must escape from a submerged, upside-down F1 cockpit in order to pass the test.

Factfile

 Guido Cappellini

This Italian started racing with karts and Formula 3. Fast racing boats took over from fast cars in 1983. Until he retired in 2009, he dominated F1 Powerboat with a record 10 championship titles.

Surviving the "big one"

In 1984 when 3.5-liter V8 engines were put into F1 boats, accidents – "big ones" – followed. Four drivers were killed in just a few months. The open boats were without gears, brakes or seatbelts.

TENNIS

The modern rules for this racquet sport were compiled in England in the 1890s, but many of the terms used (for example, "love" for zero) are French. Millions follow the Grand Slams (Majors). There are events for individuals (singles) and pairs (doubles). A tennis court can have a hard, clay or grass surface, and all aspects of the game, like net height and ball size, are regulated. Each game starts with a serve, and players alternate serving. A game is won when one player has at least four points with a two-point margin. There is a minimum of six games in a set. Women's matches consist of three sets, and men's, of five. The player or pair who wins the most sets in a match is the winner.

> "Tennis is a perfect combination of violent action taking place in an atmosphere of total tranquility."
>
> Billie Jean King, winner of 39 Grand Slams

All-Stars

Roger Federer

1998–   Switzerland

Federer holds the record for the most Grand Slam singles titles (20). He has 33 ATP World Tour awards and has spent a total 302 weeks ranked No. 1. He is fast, a tactician, and can produce winning shots from anywhere on the court.

Serena Williams

1995–   USA

The younger of the powerhouse Williams sisters has won 23 singles, 14 doubles and two mixed doubles Grand Slam titles. (Her trophy case also holds four Olympic golds.) Her serves are ferociously fast, powerful and accurate.

Rafael Nadal

2001–   Spain

His dominance of the clay court earned Nadal the nickname "The King of Clay." He has won 16 Grand Slam singles titles, 49 ATP titles and an Olympic gold. His game is high energy and his edge is his unwavering competitiveness.

▼ Grand Slam (Majors) tournaments

The four events in the Grand Slam calendar are the Australian Open (January), French Open (May/June), Wimbledon (June/July) and US Open (August/September). The total prize money for the four Grand Slams currently amounts to $180 million! No wonder they attract the best tennis players in the world and massive TV audiences.

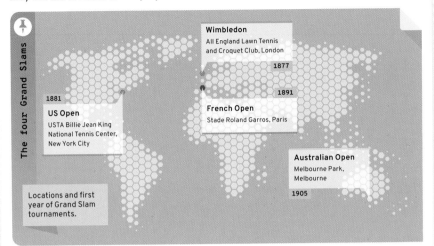

The four Grand Slams

Wimbledon All England Lawn Tennis and Croquet Club, London — 1877

US Open USTA Billie Jean King National Tennis Center, New York City — 1881

French Open Stade Roland Garros, Paris — 1891

Australian Open Melbourne Park, Melbourne — 1905

Locations and first year of Grand Slam tournaments.

10-plus Grand Slam singles titles

🧍	🏳	📅	🏆
Men			
Roger Federer	SUI	2003–2018	20
Rafael Nadal	ESP	2005–2017	17
Pete Sampras	USA	1990–2002	14
Novak Djokovic	SRB	2008–2018	13
Roy Emerson	AUS	1961–1967	12
Rod Laver	AUS	1960–1969	11
Björn Borg	SWE	1974–1981	11
Bill Tilden	USA	1920–1930	10
Women			
Margaret Court	AUS	1960–1973	24
Serena Williams	USA	1999–2017	23
Steffi Graf	GER	1987–1999	22
Helen Wills Moody	USA	1923–1938	19
Chris Evert	USA	1974–1986	18
Martina Navratilova	USA	1978–1990	18
Billie Jean King	USA	1968–1975	12

Calendar Grand Slam* winners

🧍	🏳	📅	🏆
Singles			
Rod Laver	AUS	1969/1962	2
Steffi Graf	GER	1988	1
Margaret Court	AUS	1970	1
Maureen Connolly	USA	1953	1
Don Budge	USA	1938	1
Doubles			
Martina Hingis	SUI	1998	1
Martina Navratilova	USA	1984	1
Pam Shriver	USA	1984	1
Maria Bueno	BRA	1960	1
Ken McGregor	AUS	1951	1
Frank Sedgman	AUS	1951	1
Mixed doubles			
Margaret Court	AUS	1963/1965	2
Owen Davidson	AUS	1967	1
Ken Fletcher	AUS	1963	1

* **Calendar Grand Slam**: when a player wins all four Grand Slams (Majors) in singles or doubles in one year.

Factfile

Rod Laver

The only player ever to have won two calendar Grand Slams in singles, this Australian, nicknamed "The Rocket," was ranked world No. 1 from 1964–1970. A left-handed player, Laver's attacking topspin lob and crosscourt speed were legend.

Steffi Graf

This German tennis player achieved a Golden Slam – winning four Grand Slams and an Olympic gold in one year (1988). She also held the No. 1 ranking for a record 377 weeks! Graf is credited with developing the aggressive baseline game that dominates current tennis.

▼ The Championships, Wimbledon

Founded in 1877, Wimbledon is the oldest and most prestigious tennis tournament. It is the only one of the Grand Slams still played on grass (perennial ryegrass). The All-England Lawn Tennis and Croquet Club consists of 19 courts, with Wimbledon finals always played on Centre Court. The player dress code is strict: white only! This rule harks back to the 1800s when sweat-soaked attire was thought unseemly.

Men's winning records

👤	🏳	📅	🏆
Winner of most singles titles			
Roger Federer	SUI	2003–2017	8
Winner of most consecutive singles titles			
William Renshaw	GBR	1881–1886	6
Winner of most doubles titles			
Todd Woodbridge	AUS	1993–2004	9
Winner of most consecutive doubles titles			
Todd Woodbridge	AUS	1993–1997	5
Mark Woodforde	AUS		
Reginald Doherty	GBR	1897–1901	5
Laurence Doherty	GBR		
Winner of most mixed doubles titles			
Leander Paes	IND	1999–2015	4
Owen Davidson	AUS	1967–1974	
Vic Seixas	USA	1953–1956	
Ken Fletcher	AUS	1963–1968	
Winner of most titles (singles, doubles, mixed)			
Laurence Doherty	GBR	1897–1906	13

Women's winning records

👤	🏳	📅	🏆
Winner of most singles titles			
Martina Navratilova	USA	1978–1990	9
Winner of most consecutive singles titles			
Martina Navratilova	USA	1982–1987	6
Winner of most doubles titles			
Elizabeth Ryan	USA	1914–1934	12
Winner of most consecutive doubles titles			
Elizabeth Ryan	USA	1919–1923	5
Suzanne Lenglen	FRA		
Winner of most mixed doubles titles			
Elizabeth Ryan	USA	1919–1932	7
Winner of most titles (singles, doubles and mixed)			
Martina Navratilova	USA	1976–2003	20
Billie Jean King	USA	1961–1979	

Martina Navratilova
Czech-born Navratilova held the No. 1 rank for over 200 weeks in both singles and doubles! In 1982 she won 90 out of 93 matches.

Factfile

🥇 Venus Rosewater Dish

This 18.75-inch-wide platter has been presented to the Wimbledon Ladies' Singles champion since 1886. Though covered with decoration, the theme is mythology, not tennis! Winners' names are engraved, and they are presented with a mini replica to keep.

"Who's Number One?"
Bjorn Borg v. John McEnroe

Borg was looking for his fifth Wimbledon title in the 1980 final, but no one told "Superbrat" McEnroe. In the fourth set tiebreak, McEnroe won a 34-point marathon. Then in the final set, the "Ice Man's" serve triumphed. It is still regarded as one of tennis's top-five matches!

Focus on the Olympics

Tennis was an official Olympic event from 1896–1924, and then from 1988–present. The break arose from a dispute over whether professional players were eligible to play. Many tennis players now rate Olympic gold on par with Grand Slam titles. Only Steffi Graf has won a Golden Slam, winning four Grand Slams and an Olympic gold in one year.

Top gold medalists*, by country

🏳	●	●	●	○
USA	21	6	12	39
GBR	17	14	12	43
France	5	6	8	19
Russia	3	3	2	8
South Africa	3	2	1	6
Spain	2	7	3	12
Germany	2	6	2	10
Switzerland	2	2	0	4
Chile	2	1	1	4

Top individual gold medalists*

👤	🏳	●
Venus Williams	USA	4
Serena Williams	USA	4
Reginald Doherty	GBR	3

* Medal tallies include singles, doubles and mixed doubles, as well as discontinued indoor tennis.

Factfile

🏆 Andy Murray

Grand Slam winner Murray won Olympic singles gold in 2012 and 2016 (the first male to win singles double golds) and mixed doubles silver in 2012. His 2012 singles win was against Novak Djokovic.

Return match
Andy Murray v. Roger Federer

Just a month after Federer beat Murray in the 2012 Wimbledon final in four sets, Murray took down the world No. 1 in the gold medal match – on the same court – in straight sets, 6–2, 6–1, 6–4!

Wheelchair Tennis

Wheelchair tennis is one of the fastest-growing wheelchair sports in the world, and is played at the four tennis Grand Slam events, the Wheelchair Tennis Masters, and the Paralympic Games. The use of wheelchairs and a two-bounce ball allowance – the second bounce can occur outside the court – are the only differences from pedestrian tennis.

Paralympic gold medalists

👤	🏳	●
🎾 **Men's singles**		
Shingo Kunieda	JPN	2
🎾 **Women's singles**		
Esther Vergeer	NED	4
🎾 **Quad* singles**		
Peter Norfolk	GBR	2
🎾 **Men's doubles**		
Stéphane Houdet	FRA	2
🎾 **Women's doubles**		
Esther Vergeer	NED	3
🎾 **Quad* doubles**		
Nick Taylor	USA	3
David Wagner	USA	3

* Quad (quadriplegic): quad athletes have upper limb/s function loss, so may tape the racquet to a hand and use an electric-powered wheelchair. All quad events are mixed gender events.

⭐ Superstar

Esther Vergeer

This wheelchair tennis player, who retired in 2013, holds seven Paralympic gold medals among her 148 singles titles. Her career record is 695 wins to 25 losses, including an unbroken winning streak of 470 singles matches! She also won the wheelchair tennis doubles Grand Slam twice.

↻ 1995–2013   🏳 Netherlands

Para Athletes

OTHER RACQUET SPORTS

In addition to tennis, racquet sports also include table tennis, badminton and squash. Singles and doubles matches are played indoors (doubles squash is usually played on a slightly wider court). All are incredibly fast paced with top badminton players hitting the shuttlecock (a feathered cone embedded in a cork or rubber base) at speeds up to 200 mph. This means the receiving player must react in microseconds. Table tennis and badminton are Olympic events, but squash is not yet included. In international tournaments, China dominates badminton and table tennis, while Egypt rules squash.

> **"People who see a professional badminton match up close are always shocked at the speed."**
>
> Rajiv Ouseph, European badminton champion (2017)

World Badminton Championships

`BWF`

Together with the Olympics, this tournament determines world badminton rankings and the world No. 1. Held every year save Olympic years, the competition takes place in locations around the world. Though sometimes called "physical chess," badminton is a tough, fast game that requires immense stamina, agility, lightning-fast reactions and strategy. A game is the first player to 21 points, and a match consists of three games.

Players with three-plus medals

		S*	D*	XD*
Men				
Lin Dan	CHN	5	0	0
Cai Yun	CHN	0	4	0
Fu Haifeng	CHN	0	4	0
Hendra Setiawan	INA	0	3	0
Park Joo-bong	KOR	0	2	3
Zhang Nan	CHN	0	1	3
Kim Dong-moon	KOR	0	1	2
Women				
Han Aiping	CHN	2	1	0
Li Lingwei	CHN	2	1	0
Zhao Yunlei	CHN	0	2	3
Gao Ling	CHN	0	3	1
Yu Yang	CHN	0	3	0
Guan Weizhen	CHN	0	3	0
Huang Sui	CHN	0	3	0
Lin Ying	CHN	0	3	0
Ge Fei	CHN	0	2	1
Liliyana Natsir	INA	0	0	4

* S=Singles, D=Doubles, XD=Mixed doubles

Factfile

 China

China dominates world badminton. Of its 1.4 billion population, over 100 million play. The Chinese teams are full of badminton stars. In three championships they won all five gold medals on offer. No other country has achieved this.

 The long, fast game
PV Sindhu v. Nozomi Okuhara

The women's singles World Championship of 2017 resulted in the second-longest match ever. For 110 minutes – including a 73-shot rally – PV Sindhu (India) slogged it out against Nozomi Okuhara (Japan), before Okuhara triumphed.

All-Stars

Lin Dan

 2000– China

"Super Dan" was the first and, to date, the only player to claim badminton's nine major international titles – a Super Grand Slam – by age 28. This Chinese player's current career tally is 615 wins and only 90 losses.

Jan-Ove Waldner

1982–2016 Sweden

This Swedish player, the "Mozart of table tennis," is revered in China for his skill. He is the only Western player to have been the world champion, and a World Cup and Olympic gold medal winner in one year (1992).

Jahangir Khan

1981–1993 Pakistan

This Pakistan squash player had a 555-match winning streak over five years and eight months – a Guinness record! He was six-time world champion and 10-time British Open Champion. The rallies of this ultra-fit athlete were long and fast.

World Open Squash Championships

`PSA`

The international squash circuit works in a similar way to tennis. There are over 200 tournaments a year with around 800 professional players representing over 60 countries. The conclusion to the series is the championship – the World Open – where the world's top-ranked male and female players compete in singles and doubles elimination matches. The prize purse for the championship amounts to $1 million.

Multiple World Open champions

		🏆	②
Men's			
Jansher Khan*	PAK	8	1
Jahangir Khan*	PAK	6	3
Geoff Hunt	AUS	4	1
Amr Shabana	EGY	4	0
Ramy Ashour	EGY	3	3
Nick Matthew	GBR	3	0
David Palmer	AUS	2	1
Women's			
Nicol David	MAS	8	0
Sarah Fitz-Gerald	AUS	5	1
Susan Devoy	AUS	4	1
Michelle Martin	AUS	3	4
Nour El Sherbini	EGY	2	2
Carol Owens	AUS	2	0
Heather McKay	AUS	2	0

*The Khan rivalry dominated squash in the 1980s.

Factfile

 Jansher Khan

Khan held the rank of world No. 1 for 12 years. During his 16-year career (1986–2001) he won 99 titles, and his lightning reflexes and speed contributed to Pakistan's 50-year dominance of the sport.

 Nicol Ann David

Nicknamed the "Duracell Bunny" for her unstoppable style of play, this Malaysian player was world No. 1 for a record 108 months (2006–2015). This included a 51-week winning streak! She remains in the world top 10.

▼ World Table Tennis Championships

ITTF

Since the first championships in 1926, this sport has been dominated, in turn, by Hungary, Japan, China and Sweden. Championships are currently held every year, and there are singles, doubles and team events. Once a highly "cat and mouse" defensive game (one rally in 1936 for the game's first point lasted for over two hours), games are now limited to 10 minutes if 18 points have not been scored.

Top singles medalists, by gold

		●	●	●	○
Men					
Viktor Barna	HUN	5	1	1	7
Women					
Angelica Rozeanu	ROM/ISR	6	0	1	7

Top doubles medalists, by gold

		●	●	●	○
Men					
Viktor Barna*	HUN	7	1	0	8
	ENG	1	1	4	6
Women					
Mária Mednyánszky	HUN	6	0	2	8
Anna Sipos	HUN	6	0	1	7

* Viktor Barna represented England between 1939–1954 in men's, mixed doubles and men's team events.

Top mixed doubles medalists, by gold

		●	●	●	○
Mária Mednyánszky	HUN	6	2	2	10

Top nations, team event

		●	●	●	○
Men					
China		21	5	3	29
Women					
China		21	5	3	29

Overall nation medal count (all events)

	●	●	●	○
China	141	101	154	396
Hungary	72	61	77	210
Japan	49	35	72	156
Czech Republic*	29	36	55	120
Romania	20	11	21	52
GBR	15	31	60	106
Sweden	14	11	15	40
USA	10	2	19	31
Austria	7	15	37	59
South Korea	5	15	40	60

* Medal tally of Czech Republic includes those of former Czechoslovakia.

Factfile

 Hungary

Table tennis has been popular in Hungary since the 1920s, and the country was important in setting up an international federation. From 1926–1939, they won the men's world championships nine times. Hungary is currently second on the overall medals table.

 Ma Long

Ma Long held the No. 1 world ranking for a record 64 months and was world and Olympic champion in 2018. He was the first male player to have won every table tennis singles title. In 2016, he had a career Grand Slam with Olympics, World Championships and World Cup wins.

A Moment in Time

Clean sweep

 China

📅 August 13–23, 2008

📍 Peking University Stadium, Beijing, China

🖱 2008 Summer Olympics

In 2012 and 2016, China had a clean sweep of the golds in table tennis, but in 2008 their podium dominance went even further. They won eight of the 12 medals, taking gold, silver and bronze in the men's and women's singles along with gold in the men's and women's team events.

Controversy ❗

Throwing the match

📅 August 1, 2012

📍 ExCeL London, England

🖱 2012 Summer Olympics

In the 2012 games, eight women's doubles table tennis players were disqualified for "not using one's best efforts to win." The players from South Korea, China and Indonesia were trying to manipulate who they played in the knockout stage. In one match, the longest rally in the first game lasted only four shots.

Para Table Tennis

In 1960, table tennis was one of eight events in the first Paralympic Games. It is the third largest Paralympic sport in terms of the number of athletes participating, from more than 100 countries. All physical and intellectual impairments are eligible for standing or wheelchair classes. A match consists of five games of 11 points with a margin of two points for the leader.

Top medal tally* countries, by gold

	●	●	●	○
China	59	26	14	99
West Germany FRG	43	28	26	97
France	34	43	47	124
Austria	29	23	29	81
GBR	26	29	42	97
South Korea	26	29	30	85
Germany	24	25	27	76
Netherlands	18	13	23	54
Sweden	16	27	23	66
Switzerland	14	7	10	31

* Medal tallies are based on the full program of men's, women's and team events.

Individual Paralympic medalists

		●	●	●	○
Zhang Xiaoling	CHN	9	1	2	12
Jochen Wollmert	GER	5	1	2	8

Superstar ★

Ibrahim Hamato

After losing both arms in a train accident, Ibrahim continued to play table tennis. To serve, he flicks the ball up with a foot and holds the racket in his mouth. A Paralympic gold has eluded this extraordinary athlete, but he has won three silver in African and Egyptian championships.

🔄 2006–   🏳 Egypt

Para Athletes

GOLF

The modern game of golf has its origins in 1764 Scotland, with St. Andrew's first 18-hole course. The aim is to hit a small, hard ball with differently shaped and weighted clubs around a nine- or 18-hole course. Play starts by teeing off, striking (driving) the ball from the tee down the fairway. Then, various shots and clubs are played to get the ball onto the green – avoiding hazards – and into the hole (cup). Par for a hole is the number of stokes a player should take to complete it. The player with the lowest score (least number of shots per hole), wins. The golfer's dream is a hole-in-one – from the tee into the hole with one stroke!

> "There is no king of golf. Never has been, never will be. Golf is the most democratic game on Earth… It punishes and exalts us all with splendid equal opportunity."
>
> Arnold Palmer, winner 62 PGA Tours

All-Stars

Jack Nicklaus

1961–2005 🚩 USA

Known as "The Golden Bear," Nicklaus won 73 PGA Tours and 18 other major titles. Noted for his long and straight hits, his 1963, 341-yard shot remained a record for 20 years. He won his final Masters title at age 46.

Tiger Woods

1996– 🚩 USA

Within a year of turning professional, Woods had won three PGA Tour events and the Masters. He was ranked No. 1 for a record number of weeks and has won 79 PGA Tour titles to date. (Back surgery has affected his game recently.)

Arnold Palmer

1954–2006 🚩 USA

Nicknamed "The King," Palmer won 62 PGA Tours, seven Majors and a slew of other titles. He, along with Jack Nicklaus and Gary Player, made golf more popular among the working class, and his fans were proud to be known as "Arnie's Army."

Record Breakers

Albatrosses* scored in men's Majors

👤	📅	⛳	⚪
Masters			
Louis Oosthuizen	2012	2	2
Jeff Maggert	1994	13	2
Bruce Devlin	1967	8	2
Gene Sarazen	1935	15	2
US Open			
Nick Watney	2012	17	2
Shaun Micheel	2010	6	2
Chen Tze-chung	1985	2	2
The Open			
Paul Lawrie	2009	7	2
Gary Evans	2004	4	2
Greg Owen	2001	11	2
Jeff Maggert	2001	6	2
Manny Zerman	2000	5	2
Bill Rogers	1983	17	2
Johnny Miller	1972	5	2
Young Tom Morris	1870	1	3
PGA			
Joey Sindelar	2006	5	2
Per-Ulrik Johansson	1995	11	2
Darrell Kestner	1993	13	2

* **Albatross (double eagle):** using three fewer shots (3 under par) than expected for a hole. The odds of an albatross are a million to one; for a hole-in-one it's 12,000 to one.

Albatrosses scored in women's Majors

👤	📅	⛳	⚪
Du Maurier Classic			
Dawn Coe-Jones	1993	4	2
British Open			
Vikki Laing	2014	17	2
Karen Stupples	2004	2	2
Åsa Gottmo	2002	7	2

Winners of the men's career Grand Slam*

👤	🚩	📚
Jack Nicklaus	USA	3
Tiger Woods	USA	3
Ben Hogan	USA	1
Gary Player	RSA	1
Gene Sarazen	USA	1

* **Career Grand Slam:** winning all four of golf's Majors (see page 35) during a golfer's career. Covers the Masters era.

Most men's Majors won in a calendar year*

👤	🚩	📅	🏆
Tiger Woods	USA	2000	US Open The Open PGA
Ben Hogan	USA	1953	Masters US Open The Open

* **Calendar year:** January 1 to December 31.

Consecutive victories at a men's Major

👤	🚩	📅	🏆
The Open			
Young Tom Morris	SCO	1868–1872*	4
Jamie Anderson	SCO	1877–1879	3
Bob Ferguson	SCO	1880–1882	3

* No Open Championship played in 1871.

Consecutive victories at a LPGA Major*

👤	🚩	📅	🏆
Titleholders Championship			
Patty Berg	USA	1937–1939	3
LPGA Championship			
Annika Sörenstam	SWE	2003–2005	3
Women's PGA Championship			
Inbee Park	KOR	2013–2015	3

50-plus wins on PGA/LPGA Tours*

👤	📅	🏆
Men		
Sam Snead	1936–1965	82
Tiger Woods	1996–2013	79
Jack Nicklaus	1962–1986	73
Ben Hogan	1938–1959	64
Arnold Palmer	1955–1973	62
Byron Nelson	1935–1951	52
Billy Casper	1956–1975	51
Women		
Kathy Whitworth	1962–1985	88
Mickey Wright	1956–1973	82
Annika Sörenstam	1995–2008	72
Louise Suggs	1946–1962	61
Patty Berg	1937–1962	60
Betsy Rawls	1951–1972	55

* The PGA and LPGA Tours organize the main tournaments (48 for the PGA; 33 for the LPGA) for professional golfers.

Solheim Cup* head to heads

	Overall	Singles	Foursomes	Fourballs
USA won	174	87	43	44
Europe won	156	60	51	45

* **Solheim Cup:** women's golf competition between a US team and a European team. It is held every two years.

Ryder Cup* head to heads

	Overall	Singles	Foursomes	Fourballs
USA won	465	235	136	94
Europe won	358	169	107	82

* **Ryder Cup:** men's golf competition between a US team and a European team. It is held every two years.

▼ The Majors

R&A/USGA

There are four tournaments that make up the Majors golf championships: the Masters Tournament, the US Open, The Open Championship (also called the British Open) and the PGA Championship. No golfer has won all four – a calendar Grand Slam – in a year. Tiger Woods came close with three Majors in 2000 and the Masters in 2001. This achievement has become known as the "Tiger Slam."

Most victories in the Majors

👤	🚩	📅	🏆
Masters* Tournament			
Jack Nicklaus	USA	1962–1986	6
US Open			
Jack Nicklaus	USA	1962–1986	4
Ben Hogan	USA	1946–1953	4
Bobby Jones	USA	1923–1930	4
Willie Anderson	SCO	1901–1905	4
The Open Championship			
Harry Vardon	JER	1896–1914	6
PGA Championship			
Jack Nicklaus	USA	1962–1986	5
Walter Hagen	USA	1914–1929	5

* The Masters, unlike other Majors, is always played at the same course, the Augusta National Golf Club, in Augusta, Georgia.

From 1860–2018, there have been 446 Majors champions. Of these, the US leads with 269, followed by Scotland with 55 – impressive, as Scotland's population is 62 times smaller!

Lowest aggregate score (four rounds)*

👤	🚩	📅	⛳
Masters Tournament			
Jordan Spieth	USA	2015	270
Tiger Woods	USA	1997	270
US Open			
Rory McIlroy	NIR	2011	268
The Open Championship			
Henrik Stenson	SWE	2016	264
PGA Championship			
David Toms	USA	2001	265

* Aggregate score: the total number of strokes taken by a player to complete four rounds in one of the Majors.

Single-round record*

👤	🚩	📅	⛳
The Open Championship			
Branden Grace	RSA	2017	62

* Single-round record: the lowest-ever scoring round (for 18 holes) in any of the Majors. Grace achieved this history-making score in the third round of the 2017 Open Championship at the Royal Birkdale Golf Club, in England.

| Factfile

Claret Jug (Gold Champion Trophy)

The Open Championship winner is awarded the Claret Jug. He holds it until the next Open, when he is given a replica jug. Until 1870, the trophy was the leather-and-silver Challenge Belt, which three-time winner Young Tom Morris finally kept.

Colin Montgomerie

This Scottish player is one of the world's top golfers not to have won any of the Majors. He has been runner-up on five occasions, coming second in three US Opens (1994, 1997, 2006) and once in both The Open (2005) and the PGA Championship (1995).

▼ Women's Majors

Five tournaments make up the LPGA Majors – the ANA Inspiration, the US Women's Open, the Women's PGA Championship, the Women's British Open and The Evian Championship. No woman has won four – let alone five – Majors in a year to claim a Grand Slam, but seven women have made career Grand Slams.

Most victories in the women's Majors*

👤	🚩	📅	🏆
Most LPGA Majors wins			
Patty Berg	USA	1937–1958	15

* Majors: since 1930 the number of Majors has increased from three to four, and then to five.

Lowest aggregate score (four rounds)

👤	🚩	📅	⛳
The Evian Championship			
Chun In-gee	KOR	2016	263

Single-round record

👤	🚩	📅	⛳
The Evian Championship			
Kim Hyo-joo	KOR	2014	61

| Factfile

Annika Sörenstam

Sörenstam, winner of 93 international tournaments, is the only woman to have shot a 59 in a competition. In 2003, this Swedish–American was invited to play in a PGA Tour – the first woman in this men's tour since 1954.

Longest official tournament
Se Ri Pak v. Jenny Chuasiriporn

After four rounds of the 1998 US Open, their scores were tied. After an 18-hole playoff, the 20-year-olds tied again. In a sudden-death playoff, Pak made an 18-foot putt to win. In total, Pak and Chuasiriporn played 92 holes!

A Moment in Time

A hole-in-one at the Postage Stamp

👤 Gene Sarazen

📅 July 11, 1973

📍 8th hole, Royal Troon, Scotland

➤ Round 1, The Open Championship

This par-3 hole earned the Postage Stamp name because of its small green. But at age 71, American Gene Sarazen sunk the ball in one shot! So perfect – or lucky – was Sarazen's shot that it missed all the deep hollow hazards. The hollows were made by World War II soldiers' hand-grenade practice.

Controversy !

Tiger Woods' illegal drop

👤 Tiger Woods

📅 April 12, 2013

📍 15th hole, Augusta National Golf Course

➤ Round 2, Masters Tournament

After Woods' third shot rebounded off the flagstick on the 15th hole and rolled into the water, Woods dropped his ball back into play, but not from the correct drop zone. Instead, he used a dry spot six feet farther back. Officials noticed the breach on TV replays, and Woods was penalized two shots.

ICE HOCKEY

The modern rules of this contact team sport were developed in Montreal, Canada, in 1875. Canada, the Czech Republic, Finland, Russia, Sweden and the USA dominate international competitions. Ice hockey is fast, aggressive and very physical. On the ice are two teams of six skaters, each trying to hit the puck (a 1x3-inch disk of vulcanized rubber) past the goaltender and into the opposing team's net to score a goal. The team with the most goals wins. The stick consists of a shaft ending with a long, wide, flat blade. With skate speeds of 20-30 mph, there is a lot of contact between players, so all wear a mouthguard, helmet and padded protective gear.

> **"What happened? Was Wayne Gretzky sick?"**
> Hall of Famer Larry Robinson after winning Player of the Week

All-Stars

Wayne Gretzky

🕐 1978–1999   🏁 Canada

The only player in NHL records to nail 200 points in a single season, Gretzky – "The Great One" – achieved this outstanding feat four times in his career! Gretzky also holds the record for scoring 50 goals in just 39 games.

Gordie Howe

🕐 1946–1980   🏁 Canada

"Mr. Hockey," like Gretzky, recorded 800-plus goals and won six MVP trophies in his 34-season career. The "Gordie Howe Hat Trick," named for Howe, is when a player records a goal, an assist and a fight in a single match!

Bobby Orr

🕐 1966–1978   🏁 Canada

Hockey's best defenseman earned eight James Norris Trophy wins, three MVPs and two Stanley Cups. He led the NHL scoring in 1970 with the Boston Bruins, and made "The Goal" that gave the Bruins their first Stanley Cup.

▼ National Hockey League

NHL

Twenty-four American and seven Canadian professional ice hockey teams compete in the NHL. Originally Canadian only, American teams joined in 1924. Teams from each conference and division play the regular season from October–April and the Stanley Cup playoffs in the post-season, April–June.

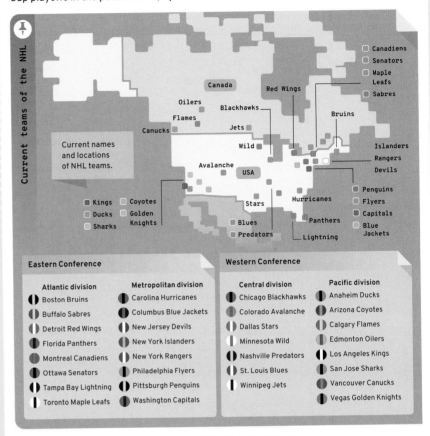

Current teams of the NHL.

Current names and locations of NHL teams.

Eastern Conference

Atlantic division
- Boston Bruins
- Buffalo Sabres
- Detroit Red Wings
- Florida Panthers
- Montreal Canadiens
- Ottawa Senators
- Tampa Bay Lightning
- Toronto Maple Leafs

Metropolitan division
- Carolina Hurricanes
- Columbus Blue Jackets
- New Jersey Devils
- New York Islanders
- New York Rangers
- Philadelphia Flyers
- Pittsburgh Penguins
- Washington Capitals

Western Conference

Central division
- Chicago Blackhawks
- Colorado Avalanche
- Dallas Stars
- Minnesota Wild
- Nashville Predators
- St. Louis Blues
- Winnipeg Jets

Pacific division
- Anaheim Ducks
- Arizona Coyotes
- Calgary Flames
- Edmonton Oilers
- Los Angeles Kings
- San Jose Sharks
- Vancouver Canucks
- Vegas Golden Knights

Stanley Cup finals record

⭐	🏆	2️⃣	📅⭐
Montreal Canadiens	24	9	1993
Toronto Maple Leafs	13	8	1967
Detroit Red Wings	11	13	2008
Boston Bruins	6	13	2011
Chicago Blackhawks	6	7	2015
Edmonton Oilers	5	2	1990
Pittsburgh Penguins	5	1	2017
New York Rangers	4	7	1994
New York Islanders	4	1	1983
New Jersey Devils	3	2	2003
Philadelphia Flyers	2	6	1975
Los Angeles Kings	2	1	2014
Colorado Avalanche	2	0	2001
Dallas Stars	1	3	1999
Calgary Flames	1	2	1989
Anaheim Ducks	1	1	2007
Carolina Hurricanes	1	1	2006
Tampa Bay Lightning	1	1	2004
Washington Capitals	1	1	2018

Factfile

✈ The wait is over
New York Rangers v. Vancouver Canucks

The 1994 NHL final attracted a record TV audience, who watched the Rangers end their 54-year championship nightmare. Tied after six games, the Rangers won 3–2 in game seven at Madison Square Garden. The Stanley Cup was finally in their hands!

🏅 Stanley Cup

Standing over 35 inches tall, this impressive trophy is awarded annually to the winner of the NHL playoffs. Montreal HC were the first recipients, in 1893. The names of the winning team are engraved on a band on the cup – when the band is full, a new one is added.

Kontinental Hockey League `KHL`

This international hockey league was started in 2008. Among its 27 members are teams from China, Russia, Finland and Kazakhstan. Like the NHL, there are conferences and divisions, a regular season and playoffs. On September 7, 2011, almost all of the Lokomotiv Yaroslavl team died in an accident on their way to the season-opening game.

Cup winners

Gagarin Cup	
Ak Bars Kazan	3
Dynamo Moscow	2
Metallurg Magnitogorsk	2
SKA Saint Petersburg	2
Salavat Yulaev Ufa	1

Continental Cup*	
CSKA Moscow	3
SKA Saint Petersburg	2
Salavat Yulaev Ufa	2
Avangard Omsk	1
Dynamo Moscow	1
Traktor Chelyabinsk	1

* **Continental Cup:** awarded to the team with the most points at the end of the regular season.

Justin Azevedo
In the 2014 final, this Ak Bars Kazan center scored a goal in all seven games.

Factfile

Gagarin Cup

Named for the first cosmonaut, Yuri Gagarin, this 33-inch-tall trophy, engraved with Gagarin's image, is presented to the KHL playoff winner. The link to Gagarin reflects Russia's growing hockey success.

Sergei Mozyakin

This Metallurg Magnitogorsk winger is the KHL's all-time highest scorer. He is the best player never to play in the NHL. He hits hard and accurately, and can predict play in advance.

Ice Hockey World Championships `IIHF`

This annual men's international ice hockey tournament consists of 16 championship teams and 24 (or more) teams in divisions I–III. Until 1968, the World Championship was part of the Olympic program. The first stand-alone event was held in 1930. Championship winners are awarded gold medals; the runners-up get silver and bronze.

Overall medal table

	●	●	●	○
Canada	26	14	9	49
Soviet Union URS	22	7	5	34
Sweden	11	19	17	47
Czechoslovakia TCH	6	12	16	34
Czech Republic	6	1	5	12
Russia	5	3	4	12
USA	2	9	8	19
Finland	2	8	3	13
GBR	1	2	2	5
Slovakia	1	2	1	4
Switzerland	0	3	8	11
Germany	0	1	2	3
West Germany FRG	0	1	0	1
Austria	0	0	2	2

The women's championships started in 1990. Canada and the US top the medal tally with 18 each, but Canada leads on gold medal wins.

Factfile

Canada

As a "Big Six" team, Canada dominated the sport until the 1960s. It returned to form with Team Canada in 1994, when it beat Italy in the championships. Since then it has triumphed six times.

Sweden

Known as *Tre Kronor* (Three Crowns), players on the current champions' team are in the Hall of Fame, and nine have won the Triple – gold in the Olympics, the World Championship and the Stanley Cup.

Focus on the Olympics

Men's ice hockey has been an Olympic event since 1920. Women's was added in 1998, and the Paralympic event in 1984. Originally purely for amateurs, the introduction of Soviet state-sponsored "amateurs" in the 1950s eventually led to the inclusion of professional players. Olympic legend Vladislav Tretiak has won three golds and one silver.

Olympic medal table, by gold

	●	●	●	○
Men				
Canada	9	4	3	16
Soviet Union URS	7	1	1	9
USA	2	8	1	11
Sweden	2	3	4	9
Czech Republic	1	0	1	2
GBR	1	0	1	2
OAR	1	0	0	1
EUN	1	0	0	1
Women				
Canada	4	2	0	6
USA	2	3	1	6

Leading gold medalists are Hayley Wickenheiser, Jayna Hefford and Caroline Ouellette (CAN) with four. Vladislav Tretiak tops the men's table with three gold medals.

Factfile

Finland

Finland has competed in Olympic ice hockey 17 times to date, but has never won the gold. The men's and women's teams have a combined two silver and seven bronze medals.

"Miracle on Ice"
USA v. Soviet Union

In the 1980 Olympics, the amateur US team played the defending – mostly professional – champions and Cold War adversaries, the Soviet Union. The Americans won 4–3 in the "Miracle on Ice" game.

Para Ice Hockey

Originally called ice sledge hockey, the para athlete version is as fast and furious as the typical. Players must have an impairment in the lower half of their body. They use sledges with a double blade that allows the puck to pass underneath. Their two sticks have a spike at one end to propel the sledge and a blade at the other to shoot the puck.

Leading medal tally, by country

	●	●	●	○
USA	4	0	1	5
Norway	1	3	1	5
Canada	1	2	2	5
Sweden	1	0	2	3
Japan	0	1	0	1
Russia	0	1	0	1
South Korea	0	0	1	1

* From 2010 onward, para ice hockey teams could include men and women athletes. To date, just a couple mixed teams have been formed.

Individual Paralympic medalists

		●	●	●	○
Helge Bjørnstad	NOR	1	3	0	4
Eskil Hagen	NOR	1	3	0	4
Atle Haglund	NOR	1	3	0	4
Kjetil Korbu Nilsen	NOR	1	3	0	4

Superstar

Brad Bowden

Bowden is one of few para athletes to have won golds at both the Winter and Summer Olympics, competing in ice hockey and wheelchair basketball (2004). On the ice, he is known for his strategic play and sledge and puck control. His ice hockey career medal tally currently stands at eight.

1999–   Canada

GYMNASTICS

The sport of gymnastics has been around for over 2,000 years. (Athletes in ancient Olympics competed in the nude!) In modern artistic gymnastics, women compete on the vault, bars, balance beam and floor. Men also do pommel horse and rings. Rhythmic gymnastics – floor routines with ribbons and other equipment – is a separate discipline for women only. Since 2000, the Olympics has also included trampoline events. Individuals and teams compete in gymnastics. The aim is to lose minimum points for poor execution, and to gain maximum points for difficult moves and meeting requirements. A world-class score is around 16 points.

> "The sport is called artistic gymnastics. So you do have to be a little bit of an actress."
>
> Simone Biles, winner four Olympic golds (2016)

All-Stars

Kōhei Uchimura

2007– | Japan

This Japanese athlete's eight-year run as world No. 1 ended in 2017 after injury meant pulling out of the World Championships. Uchimura was the first to win every major all-around title twice. He is considered a master of all gymnastic events.

Nadia Comăneci

1971–1984 | Romania

Perhaps the most famous gymnast of all time, this Romanian athlete made Olympic history when she scored a perfect 10 in the uneven bars at the 1976 Montreal Games. She went on to score eight more 10s in the 1976 and 1980 games.

George Eyser

1904–1909 | USA

In the 1904 Olympics in St. Louis, Missouri, Eyser won six medals, including three golds in one day, as part of the US gymnastic squad – an extraordinary feat made even more impressive by the fact that Eyser had a wooden leg.

Record Breakers

World Championship* medalists, by gold

		🥇	🥈	🥉	◯
Men					
Vitaly Scherbo	URS EUN BLR	12	7	4	23
Kōhei Uchimura	JPN	10	5	4	19
Joseph Martinez	FRA	10	1	0	11
Yuri Korolyov	URS	9	3	1	13
Dmitry Bilozerchev	URS	8	4	0	12
Li Xiaopeng	CHN	8	2	1	11
Marian Drăgulescu	ROM	8	2	0	10
Chen Yibing	CHN	8	0	0	8
Eizō Kenmotsu	JPN	7	5	3	15
Alexander Dityatin	URS	7	2	3	12
Akinori Nakayama	JPN	7	2	3	12
Women					
Simone Biles	USA	10	2	2	14
Svetlana Khorkina	RUS	9	8	3	20
Larisa Latynina	URS	9	4	1	14
Gina Gogean	ROM	9	2	4	15
Ludmilla Tourischeva	URS	7	2	2	11
Daniela Silivaș	ROM	7	2	1	10
Vlasta Děkanová	TCH	7	0	0	7
Simona Amânar	ROM	6	4	0	10
Nellie Kim	URS	5	4	2	11
Yelena Shushunova	URS	5	4	2	11

* **World Championships:** held (annually or biennially) in each gymnastic discipline – artistic, rhythmic, trampolining, acrobatic and aerobic.

Perfect 10s* at the Olympic Games

		🎚
Men		
Li Ning	CHN	5
Dmitry Bilozerchev	RUS	4
Tong Fei	CHN	4
Koji Gushiken	JPN	3
Lou Yun	CHN	3
Shinji Morisue	JPN	3
Peter Vidmar	USA	3
Bart Conner	USA	3
Vladimir Artemov	RUS	2
Mitch Gaylord	USA	2
Zoltán Magyar	HUN	2
Women		
Nadia Comăneci	ROM	9
Daniela Silivaș	ROM	7
Yelena Shushunova	RUS	7
Julianne McNamara	USA	5
Ecaterina Szabo	ROM	4
Ma Yanhong	CHN	3
Mary Lou Retton	USA	3
Dagmar Kersten	GDR	2
Nellie Kim	URS	2

* **Perfect 10:** a score of 10 out of 10 points. The scoring system changed in 2006, making a perfect 10 no longer possible.

Most successful* individual gymnasts

		🥇
Men		
Floor exercise		
Marian Drăgulescu	ROM	4
Vault		
Marian Drăgulescu	ROM	4
Horizontal bar		
Epke Zonderland	NED	3
Zou Kai	CHN	3
Takashi Ono	JPN	3
Leon Štukelj	YUG	3
Parallel bars		
Li Xiaopeng	CHN	4
Vladimir Artemov	URS	4
Pommel horse		
Zoltán Magyar	HGY	5
Miroslav Cerar	YUG	5
Still rings		
Jury Chechi	ITA	6
All-around individual – artistic gymnastics		
Kōhei Uchimura	JPN	6
Women		
Floor exercise		
Simone Biles	USA	4
Larisa Latynina	URS	4
Vault		
Věra Čáslavská	TCH	4
Beam		
Daniela Silivaș	ROM	3
Nadia Comăneci	ROM	3
Uneven bars		
Svetlana Khorkina	RUS	7
All-around individual – artistic gymnastics		
Simone Biles	USA	4
Larisa Latynina	URS	4

* **Successful:** gymnasts with the most golds in each discipline, combined Olympics and World Championships.

Most successful all-around teams*

	🥇	🥈	🥉	◯
Men				
China	14	6	4	24
Women				
Soviet Union	20	3	0	23

* **All-around teams:** the national teams with the most golds, combined Olympics and World Championships (from first event to 2017) in multiple artistic gymnastic disciplines.

In all-around individual events in artistic gymnastics, men compete in six disciplines and women in four. There is also an all-around event for rhythmic gymnastics.

Focus on the Olympics

Artistic gymnastics attracts huge audiences and ranks as one of the most-watched Olympic events. The men's events have been included since 1896, though events like rope climbing, Indian clubs and tumbling have disappeared. There are now six events for men. First demonstrated at the 1928 Olympics, the current four women's events appeared in 1952.

Artistic gymnastics all-time medal leaders, by gold

👤	🚩	🔄	🏆	●	●	●	○
Men							
Sawao Kato	JPN	1968–1977	1968, 1972, 1976	8	3	1	12
Nikolai Andrianov	URS	1971–1980	1972, 1976, 1980	7	5	3	15
Boris Shakhlin	URS	1954–1966	1956, 1960, 1964	7	4	2	13
Viktor Chukarin	URS	1952–1956	1952, 1956	7	3	1	11
Akinori Nakayama	JPN	1966–1972	1968, 1972	6	2	2	10
Vitaly Scherbo	URS EUN BLR	1990–1997	1992, 1996	6	0	4	10
Takashi Ono	JPN	1952–1964	1952, 1956, 1960, 1964	5	4	4	13
Mitsuo Tsukahara	JPN	1962–1977	1968, 1972, 1976	5	1	3	9
Yukio Endo	JPN	1960–1968	1960, 1964, 1968	5	2	0	7
Alexei Nemov	RUS	1993–2004	1996, 2000, 2004	4	2	6	12
Georges Miez	SUI	1924–1936	1924, 1928, 1932, 1936	4	3	1	8
Women							
Larisa Latynina	URS	1954–1966	1956, 1960, 1964	9	5	4	18
Věra Čáslavská	TCH	1958–1968	1960, 1964, 1968	7	4	0	11
Ágnes Keleti	HUN	1937–1958	1952, 1956	5	3	2	10
Polina Astakhova	URS	1956–1968	1956, 1960, 1964	5	2	3	10
Nadia Comăneci	ROM	1971–1984	1976, 1980	5	3	1	9
Nellie Kim	URS	1969–1980	1976, 1980	5	1	0	6
Ludmilla Tourischeva	URS	1967–1977	1968, 1972, 1976	4	3	2	9
Olga Korbut	URS	1969–1977	1972, 1976	4	2	0	6
Ecaterina Szabo	ROM	1983–1987	1984	4	1	0	5
Simone Biles	USA	2013–	2016	4	0	1	5

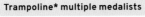

Rhythmic gymnastics* multiple medalists

👤	🚩	●	●	●	○
Yevgeniya Kanaeva	RUS	2	0	0	2
Alina Kabaeva	RUS	1	0	1	2
Anna Bessonova	UKR	0	0	2	2

* **Rhythmic gymnastics:** the Olympic program in this discipline is for women only and combines classical ballet, apparatus work and rhythmic exercises.

Trampoline* multiple medalists

👤	🚩	●	●	●	○
Rosannagh MacLennan	CAN	2	0	0	2
He Wenna	CHN	1	0	1	2
Karen Cockburn	CAN	0	2	1	3
Huang Shanshan	CHN	0	1	1	2

* **Trampoline:** men and women do compulsory and optional routines, and are scored on difficulty, execution and time of flight.

Factfile

⭐ Soviet Union

This national women's team dominated gymnastics from its first appearance in 1952 until the Soviet Union's collapse in 1991. A tremendous amount of money and resources went toward the team, including its most-medaled gymnast, Larisa Latynina.

🏆 Simone Biles

As part of the "Final Five" 2016 US Olympic team, Biles won four golds and one bronze. In the preceding three World Championships, she took home 10 golds, two silver and two bronze. She is America's most-medaled gymnast of all time.

A Moment in Time

Perfect 10

👤 Nadia Comăneci

📅 1976

📍 Olympic Games, Moscow

➤ Artistic gymnastics

A score of 10 was thought impossible in gymnastics until Nadia Comăneci's feat in 1976. The scoreboard couldn't even display it – it appeared as 1.00. The age of the perfect 10 had passed by 1988, and under the current scoring system, there is no such thing as a "perfect" score.

Controversy

The underage Chinese gymnast

👤 Dong Fangxiao

📅 2000

📍 Olympic Games, Sydney

➤ Artistic gymnastics

Dong Fangxiao lost her medal when it was discovered that she was only 14 when she competed. Since 1997, athletes must turn 16 during their Olympic year in order to compete. When Fangxiao's points were subtracted, the Chinese team lost the bronze medal position and the US moved up from fourth to third.

Sporting Arenas

Olympic Gymnastics Arena

This venue hosted the 1988 Olympic gymnastics events. Its self-supporting cable roof was the first of its kind in the world. Recently renovated, the roof now resembles a whirling tornado.

👥 15,000   🔨 1986   📍 Seoul, South Korea

Tokyo Metropolitan Gymnasium

Shaped like a samurai's helmet, its aluminum-clad roof catches the sun at every time of day. Most of the arena's space is below ground. Originally built in 1952, it welcomed the 1964 Olympic Games.

👥 10,000   🔨 1954   📍 Tokyo, Japan

North Greenwich Arena

At the time of the 2012 Olympics, this gymnastics venue was known as the O2. Constructed like a tent, the domed roof was built on the ground and then lifted up. The arena was built around the roof.

👥 20,000   🔨 2007   📍 London, UK

SWIMMING

Freestyle (front crawl), backstroke, breaststroke and butterfly are the four competitive swimming strokes. There are individual and teams-of-four competitions over 50–1,500-meter distances. A medley race uses each of the four strokes. The only swimming event not held in a 50-meter pool is the 10-km open-water marathon. Though the strokes have changed little over recent decades, the dolphin kick was introduced in the 1988 Olympics. This kick maximizes the swimmer's diving and flip-turn speed. Before a competition, swimmers remove exposed hair and the top layer of dead skin in order to cut milliseconds off their time.

> "The water is your friend. You don't have to fight with water, just share the same spirit as the water, and it will help you move."
>
> Aleksandr Popov, winner four Olympic golds (1992, 1996)

All-Stars

Michael Phelps
🕐 2000–2016   🏳 USA

This Team USA swimmer won 23 golds, three silver and two bronze over five Olympic Games. At the 2008 Beijing Games, he won eight golds. Nicknamed the "Flying Fish," he is the most decorated Olympian of all time and holds multiple world records.

Mark Spitz
🕐 1965–1972   🏳 USA

In 1972, this celebrated American swimmer won seven Olympic golds and set seven world records. His career gold-medal haul was nine. By the time he was 10, Spitz already held 17 national records and one world record!

Dara Torres
🕐 1981–2012   🏳 USA

This American swimmer amassed 12 Olympic medals, winning one or more at each of her five Olympics. In 2008, 41-year-old Torres broke a 100-year-record: the oldest swimmer to medal at an Olympic Games.

Record Breakers

All records set on the long course in 50-meter pool.

Men's individual World Records

Freestyle			
50 m	César Cielo	BRA	20.91
100 m	César Cielo	BRA	46.91
200 m	Paul Biedermann	GER	1:42.00
400 m	Paul Biedermann	GER	3:40.07
800 m	Zhang Lin	CHN	7:32.12
1,500 m	Sun Yang	CHN	14:31.02
Backstroke			
50 m	Liam Tancock	GBR	24.04
100 m	Ryan Murphy	USA	51.85
200 m	Aaron Peirsol	USA	1:51.92
Breaststroke			
50 m	Adam Peaty	GBR	25.95
100 m	Adam Peaty	GBR	57.13
200 m	Ippei Watanabe	JPN	2:06.67
Butterfly			
50 m	Rafael Muñoz	ESP	22.43
100 m	Michael Phelps	USA	49.82
200 m	Michael Phelps	USA	1:51.51
Medley*			
200 m	Ryan Lochte	USA	1:54.00
400 m	Michael Phelps	USA	4:03.84

Women's individual World Records

Freestyle			
50 m	Sarah Sjöström	SWE	23.67
100 m	Sarah Sjöström	SWE	51.71
200 m	Federica Pellegrini	ITA	1:52.98
400 m	Katie Ledecky	USA	3:56.46
800 m	Katie Ledecky	USA	8:04.79
1,500 m	Katie Ledecky	USA	15:20.48
Backstroke			
50 m	Zhao Jing	CHN	27.06
100 m	Kylie Masse	CAN	58.10
200 m	Missy Franklin	USA	2:04.06
Breaststroke			
50 m	Lilly King	USA	29.40
100 m	Lilly King	USA	1:04.13
200 m	Rikke Møller Pedersen	DEN	2:19.11
Butterfly			
50 m	Sarah Sjöström	SWE	24.43
100 m	Sarah Sjöström	SWE	55.48
200 m	Liu Zige	CHN	2:01.81
Medley*			
200 m	Katinka Hosszú	HUN	2:06.12
400 m	Katinka Hosszú	HUN	4:26.36

*** Medley:** swimmers complete laps in freestyle, breaststroke, backstroke and butterfly.

Men's relay World Records

Freestyle			
4×100 m	Michael Phelps Garrett Weber-Gale Cullen Jones Jason Lezak	USA	3:08.24
4×200 m	Michael Phelps Ricky Berens David Walters Ryan Lochte	USA	6:58.55
Medley			
4×100 m	Aaron Peirsol Eric Shanteau Michael Phelps David Walters	USA	3:27.28

Women's relay World Records

Freestyle			
4×100 m	Shayna Jack Bronte Campbell Emma McKeon Cate Campbell	AUS	3:30.05
4×200 m	Yang Yu Zhu Qianwei Liu Jing Pang Jiaying	CHN	7:42.08
Medley			
4×100 m	Kathleen Baker Lilly King Kelsi Worrell Simone Manuel	USA	3:51.55

Mixed relay World Records

Freestyle			
4×100 m	Caeleb Dressel Nathan Adrian Mallory Comerford Simone Manuel	USA	3:19.60
Medley			
4×100 m	Matt Grevers Lilly King Caeleb Dressel Simone Manuel	USA	3:38.56

Multiple World Record* holding countries

	Men	Women	Mixed relay
USA	9	8	2
China	2	3	
Sweden		4	
GBR	3		
Brazil	2		
Germany	2		
Hungary		2	

* FINA records updated to June 21, 2018. These records were set in a 50-meter pool between 2009–2018.

World Open Water Swimming Championships

Until 2010, the open water swim championship was raced over distances of 5, 10 and 25 km, but since 2007, the 10-km race has become the main annual event. It was added to the Olympics in 2008, with the fastest time to date 1:49:55.1. Training for a race involves swimming over 80 kilometers (almost 50 miles) a week! UltraMarathon series races exceed 15 km.

Multiple medal* winners, by gold

		●	●	●	○
Men					
Thomas Lurz	GER	12	4	4	20
Yuri Kudinov	RUS	5	2	1	8
Vladimir Dyatchin	RUS	3	3	4	10
Women					
Larisa Ilchenko	RUS	8	1	0	9
Edith van Dijk	NED	6	5	4	15
Viola Valli	ITA	5	2	1	8
Britta Kamrau-Corestein	GER	4	2	4	10
Ana Marcela Cunha	BRA	3	2	5	10
Aurélie Muller	FRA	3	2	0	5

* Includes individual and team events 2000–2017.

Ilchenko developed hypothermia at the 2010 Championships in the 18.5°C waters of Lac St-Jean, Quebec, Canada. She retired soon after.

Factfile

Thomas Lurz

Known as the "godfather of German distance swimming," Lurz won 12 medals at the World Championships and bronze and silver at the Olympics (2008, 2012). Lurz still swims 3,500 km a year in training, but retired in 2015.

Edith van Dijk

The Dutch swimmer's first victory was silver in the 25-km at the 1995 European Championships. From then on, van Dijk was on the podium in 5-, 10- and 25-km races. Her longest open water swim was 88 km; she finished in 7 hrs., 45 mins.

Sporting Arenas

Indiana University Natatorium

Regarded as the fastest pool in the world, this 50-meter indoor pool has hosted Olympic trials and national and international events. 101 US records and 15 world records have been set here.

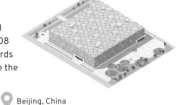

👥 4,700   🏊 1982   📍 Indianapolis, Indiana

National Aquatics Center

Known as the "Water Cube" because of its bubble-covered exterior, it was host to the 2008 Olympics, where over 25 records were broken, and will welcome the 2022 Winter Olympics.

👥 6,000   🏊 2004-7   📍 Beijing, China

Olympia Schwimmhalle

American Mark Spitz won seven gold medals here in 1972, and 20 world and 29 Olympic records were broken. In addition to the swimming, the pool hosted diving, water polo and the pentathlon swim.

👥 1,500   🏊 1972   📍 Munich, Germany

A Moment in Time

Australia wins the 100-meter relay

🏳 Australia

📅 September 16, 2000

📍 Olympic Games, Sydney

↗ Men's 4x100-meter freestyle relay

The US had never lost a men's 4x100-meter Olympic relay until the Australians came along. Michael Klim, Chris Fydler, Ashley Callus and Ian Thorpe won gold, and stole the world record. At the end of the race, Klim played air guitar, mocking the Americans' promise to "smash the Aussies like guitars."

Controversy

The body-length LZR Racer

📅 August 9–17, 2008

📍 Olympic Games, Beijing

↗ Swimming competitions

The Speedo hi-tech LZR Racer suits could reduce times by 1.9–2.2%. At the 2008 Olympics, LZR-clad swimmers won 98% of the medals and broke 25 world records. Many said the LZR was equal to "technical doping," and in 2009, the body-length suit was banned by the sports' governing body.

Para Swimming

There are individual, team and medley events for freestyle, breaststroke, butterfly and backstroke. Para swimmers may have physical, visual or intellectual impairments, and may start a race from a starting platform or from in the water. Visually impaired swimmers wear blackened goggles to assure fair competition and have an aide who "taps" them to warn that the pool end is near.

Paralympic medal leaders, by gold

		●	●	●	○
Men					
Michael Edgson*	CAN	18	0	0	18
Mike Kenny	GBR	16	2	0	18
Matthew Cowdrey	AUS	13	7	3	23
Erling Trondsen	NOR	13	6	1	20
David Roberts	GBR	11	4	1	16
Uri Bergman	ISR	11	0	1	12
Daniel Dias	BRA	10	4	1	15
Women					
Trischa Zorn	USA	41	9	4	54
Béatrice Hess	FRA	20	5	0	25
Mayumi Narita	JPN	15	3	2	20
Erin Popovich	USA	14	5	0	19
Claudia Hengst	FRG	13	4	8	25
Natalie du Toit	RSA	13	2	0	15
Elizabeth Scott	USA	10	2	5	17

* At three Paralympics, Edgson won the gold in every individual event in which he competed except one!

Superstar ⭐

Trischa Zorn

The most decorated Paralympian of all time, Zorn – blind since birth – has 54 medals, including 41 golds from seven games (1980–2004). At the 1992 games, she won 10 golds! Zorn excelled in all strokes – freestyle, breaststroke, butterfly and backstroke.

🔄 1980–2004   🏳 USA

DIVING

At its simplest, diving is about jumping or falling from a distance above the water, sometimes doing acrobatic moves during the fall. A diver can leave the board from a forward- or backward-standing position, a run up or an armstand. Points are given for the difficulty and execution of the twists, rotations, multiple somersaults, pikes (body bent at the waist with legs held straight and tight to the body) and tucks (body bent at the knees and waist with thighs held to the chest). But how the body enters the water is crucial – ideally the diver is totally vertical with arms extended over the ears and hands clasped together when they hit the water, so that there is no splash on entry.

> "Diving is... throwing yourself in the air, fighting mentally and physically to twist, turn and contort your body, before you hit the water below."
>
> Anonymous

Focus on the Olympics

Originally divided into plain diving and fancy diving, the sport made its first appearance in 1904, with the women's competition added in 1912. While some 1904 dives resembled the somersaults and twists of today's events, there was also a "plunge for distance" event, in which the diver who covered the greatest distance underwater (propelled only by his original dive), won. Since it wasn't a spectator sport, it was dropped!

Multiple medal winners, by gold*

		●	●	●	○
Men					
Greg Louganis	USA	4	1	0	5
Klaus Dibiasi	ITA	3	2	0	5
Xiong Ni	CHN	3	1	1	5
Qin Kai	CHN	2	1	2	5
Tian Liang	CHN	2	1	1	4
Pete Desjardins	USA	2	1	0	3
Robert Webster	USA	2	0	0	2
Women					
Wu Minxia	CHN	5	1	1	7
Chen Ruolin	CHN	5	0	0	5
Guo Jingjing	CHN	4	2	0	6
Fu Mingxia	CHN	4	1	0	5
Patricia McCormick	USA	4	0	0	4
Ingrid Krämer	GER	3	1	0	4
Dorothy Poynton-Hill	USA	2	1	1	4
Gao Min	CHN	2	0	0	2

* Includes medals won in individual and synchronized events.

Factfile

Wu Minxia

This Chinese diver amassed 23 gold, 11 silver and three bronze medals at Olympic Games, World Championships, World Cups and Asian Games. Wu, whose career covered 2001–2016, was named FINA Female Diver of the Year twice.

Team USA

Team USA was the team to beat from 1904 until the Chinese reentered the scene in 1984. On the Olympic medal table, the US's 49 golds still beats China's 40, and since 2008, the US squad has started to gain back ground on their diving rivals.

All-Stars

 Greg Louganis

 1976–1988   🏴 USA

Over three Olympic Games, this American diver won five medals and received some of the highest scores in diving history. At the 1982 World Championships, Louganis' 2½ pike scored perfect 10s from all judges. He holds five World Championship golds.

 Guo Jingjing

 1998–2011   🏴 China

This one- and three-meter springboard and three-meter synchronized diver has won 11 World Championship and six Olympic medals. Like other divers, Guo – "The Princess of Diving" – has poor eyesight due to impact pressure.

 Dmitri Sautin

1991–2010   🏴 Russia

In this Russian diver's five Olympic Games he won eight medals in the three- and ten-meter springboard and platform events, in both the individual and pairs events. Sautin's style was dynamic and powerful.

▼ World Championships in diving

FINA

Held as part of the World Aquatics Championships, there are men's, women's and mixed events in one-, three- and ten-meter springboard and platform diving. Divers enter as individuals, and in pairs for synchronized diving. Since 2013, there are also 27-meter (men) and 20-meter (women) high-diving events. Divers score points for level of difficulty, execution, body position and entry into the water.

Multiple medal winners, by gold*

		●	●	●	○
Men					
Qin Kai	CHN	7	0	0	7
Dmitri Sautin	RUS	5	1	3	9
He Chong	CHN	5	1	1	7
Greg Louganis	USA	5	0	0	5
Wang Feng	CHN	4	1	1	6
Qiu Bo	CHN	4	1	0	5
Women					
Guo Jingjing	CHN	10	1	0	11
Wu Minxia	CHN	8	5	1	14
Chen Ruolin	CHN	6	3	1	10
Shi Tingmao	CHN	6	1	0	7
He Zi	CHN	4	2	1	7

* Includes individual and synchronized events 1973–2017.

At the 2012 Olympics, He Zi and Wu Minxia won gold in the synchronized dive. They repeated Wu Minxia's success in the two previous Olympics with Guo Jingjing.

Factfile

Qin Kai

This Chinese three-meter springboard and synchronized diver has won a record seven golds in World Championships (2007–2015). At the 2016 Olympics, he proposed to his girlfriend and fellow diver He Zi after she won silver in her event.

China

This country's diving teams, especially the women (they occupy the top-five medal ranks), have ruled the championships since the 1980s. China tops the gold-medal chart with 83. The runners-up, Russia and the US, have a mere 13 golds!

OTHER POOL SPORTS

At the Olympics and other major international tournaments, the only other pool events are water polo and artistic dance (synchronized swimming). Both sports require immense strength, stamina and control. Water polo – originally called water rugby – is a contact sport, but ear protectors are the only safety gear. The aim for each team of six (plus a goalkeeper) is to score goals in the opponent's floating net. The first "water ballet" competition, held in 1891, was for men only, but it was women who made synchronized swimming popular. Currently, only women can compete at the Olympics in this event.

> **"When you think that your legs are strong – do more. You will dominate this game if your legs are the strongest in the pool."**
>
> Igor Milanovic, former water polo player and coach

All-Stars

Dezső Gyarmati

1952–1962 — Hungary

This legendary Hungarian water polo player was a three-time Olympic champion. Gyarmati was fast and could play any position. His team won the infamous "Blood in the Water" match (1956) between Hungary and the Soviet Union.

Oliver Halassy

1928–1938 — Hungary

Halassy won three medals in three Olympics with the Hungarian water polo team. He was also a 1,500-meter freestyle champion and the first disabled swimmer – a leg was amputated after an accident – to compete in an Olympics.

Anastasia Davydova

2001–2012 — Russia

Davydova won five gold medals at three Olympics and 11 at World Championships in duet and team synchronized swimming. In 2008, she and duet partner Anastasia Ermakova received perfect scores.

Focus on the Olympics

Water Polo

This challenging sport has been in the Olympics since 1900 (the women's game debuted in 2000). A game consists of four seven-minute periods, with only the goalkeeper allowed to touch the pool floor or use two hands on the ball. Field players tread water, pass the ball one-handed and dribble, while swimming with their heads out of the water.

Water polo team medalists, by gold

	●	●	●	○
Men				
Hungary	9	3	3	15
GBR	4	0	0	4
Yugoslavia YUG	3	4	0	7
Italy	3	2	3	8
Soviet Union URS	2	2	3	7
Germany	1	2	0	3
Croatia	1	2	0	3
Spain	1	1	0	2
France	1	0	3	4
Serbia	1	0	2	3
Women				
USA	2	2	1	5
Italy	1	1	0	2
Australia	1	0	2	3
Netherlands	1	0	0	1

The most goals scored in Olympics tournament play by a woman is 21 (Maggie Steffens, USA) and by a man, 34 (Manuel Estiarte, ESP).

Factfile

 Hungary

This is Hungary's national sport and a source of great pride. The men's team have won medals at most Olympics, and between 1932–1976 won six golds. Since the 2000 games, they've come back to win three more.

"Blood in the Water" match
Hungary v. Soviet Union (URS)

In 1956 Hungary was struggling against Soviet rule at home and in the Olympic pool. This match earned its gruesome name when a Hungarian player emerged from the pool bleeding after a Soviet-thrown punch. Hungary won 4–0.

Synchronized Swimming World Championships

 FINA

Now renamed artistic swimming, this sport combines swimming, dance and gymnastics. Individuals, pairs and teams, wearing nose clips to prevent water going into the nose, perform two–four-minute routines to music while treading water and holding their breath for up to one minute. Swimmers are penalized if they touch the pool floor. Moves in artistic swimming include lifts, rotations, spins, descents and thrusts.

Multiple individual medal winners, by gold

		●	●	●	○
Natalia Ishchenko	RUS	19	2	0	21
Svetlana Romashina	RUS	18	0	0	18
Anastasia Davydova	RUS	13	1	0	14
Svetlana Kolesnichenko	RUS	13	0	0	13
Alexandra Patskevich	RUS	13	0	0	13
Alla Shishkina	RUS	11	0	0	11
Angelika Timanina	RUS	11	0	0	11
Elvira Khasyanova	RUS	10	0	0	10
Mariya Gromova	RUS	9	0	0	9
Anastasiya Yermakova	RUS	8	2	0	10

All-time team medal winners, by gold

	●	●	●	○
Russia	51	6	0	57
USA	14	9	6	29
Canada	8	10	8	26
France	3	2	2	7
Japan	2	14	28	44

Factfile

 Huang Xuechen

Huang's career began in 2007, but despite collecting 15 silver and four bronze medals in international competition, gold has so far eluded Huang. Testament to the rigors of this sport, she carried wrist injuries for 11 years.

Russia

At the 2013 World Championships, the Russian team won every gold in artistic swimming. It was the team's seventh victory in a row. Their Olympic success is similar. Even though Natalia Ishchenko has retired, the medals keep coming.

ROWING

Rowing, in which an individual or team propels a boat, called a racing shell, along a still body of water to the end of a course, became a competitive sport in the 10th century. In sweep, each rower has one oar; in sculls, two oars. The oars are held in fixed positions. The standard World Championship distance is 2,000 meters, which can be completed in 5.5–7.5 minutes. Possibly the most famous rowing event is the annual Boat Race on the River Thames, England, between Oxford and Cambridge Universities. Training at the elite level is intense, done outdoors in all weather, and requires a six-days-a-week commitment prior to competition.

> "Eight hearts must beat as one in an eight-oared shell or you don't have a crew!"
>
> George Pocock (1911–1976), designer and builder of racing rowing shells

All-Stars

Steve Redgrave

1980–2000   GBR

Considered the most successful rower in Olympic history, Redgrave won five gold medals in the coxless pairs and coxed fours in five Olympics. He also triumphed multiple times in World Championships and Commonwealth Games.

Elisabeta Lipă

1980–2004   Romania

The most decorated female rower in Olympic history, Romanian Lipă competed in six games (1988–2004). She rowed in single and double sculls and eight-oared boats, and also earned a slew of World Championship medals.

Georgeta Damian

1997–2008   Austria

Like Redgrave and Lipă, Damian won five golds in Olympic rowing – coxless pairs and coxed eights – but she achieved this in just three Olympics, representing Romania. Damian also medaled in six World Rowing Championships.

Record Breakers

All records set over the international rowing distance of 2,000 m.

World Records, men's open water rowing

⏱		🚩
6:30.74	**Single sculls** Robert Manson	NZL
6:08.50	**Coxless pairs** Hamish Bond, Eric Murray	NZL
6:33.26	**Coxed pairs** Hamish Bond, Eric Murray, Caleb Shepherd (coxswain)	NZL
5:59.72	**Double sculls** Martin Sinković, Valent Sinković	CRO
5:37.86	**Coxless four** Andrew Triggs Hodge, Pete Reed Tom James, Alex Gregory*	GBR
5:58.96	**Coxed four** Matthias Ungemach, Bahne Rabe, Armin Eichholz, Armin Weyrauch, Joerg Dederding (coxswain)	GER
5:32.26	**Quad sculls** Artem Morozov, Oleksandr Nadtoka, Dmytro Mikhay, Ivan Dovgodko	UKR
5:18.68	**Eight** Johannes Weissenfeld, Hannes Ocik, Felix Wimberger, Maximilian Planer, Torben Johannesen, Jakob Schneider, Malte Jakschik, Richard Schmidt, Martin Sauer (coxswain)	GER

* Three of the rowers in this coxless four were victorious Oxford or Cambridge Boat Race veterans.

World Records, women's open water rowing

⏱		🚩
7:07.71	**Single sculls** Rumyana Neykova	BUL
6:49.08	**Coxless pairs** Grace Prendergast, Kerri Gowler	NZL
6:37.31	**Double sculls** Olympia Aldersey, Sally Kehoe	AUS
6:14.36	**Coxless four** Grace Prendergast, Kayla Pratt Kerri Gowler, Kelsey Bevan	NZL
6:06.84	**Quad sculls** Carina Baer, Julia Lier, Annekatrin Thiele, Lisa Schmidla	GER
5:54.16	**Eight** Amanda Polk, Kerry Simmonds, Emily Regan, Lauren Schmetterling, Grace Luczak, Caroline Lind, Victoria Opitz, Heidi Robbins, Katelin Snyder (coxswain)	USA

World Records, men's lightweight* rowing

⏱		🚩
6:43.37	**Single sculls** Marcello Miani	ITA
6:22.91	**Coxless pairs** Simon Niepmann, Lucas Tramèr	SUI
6:05.36	**Double sculls** John Smith, James Thompson	RSA
5:43.16	**Coxless four** Kasper Winther Jørgensen, Jacob Larsen, Jacob Barsøe, Morten Jørgensen	DEN
5:42.75	**Quad sculls** Georgios Konsolas, Spyridon Giannaros, Panagiotis Magdanis, Eleftherios Konsolas	GRC
5:30.24	**Eight** Klaus Altena, Christian Dahlke, Bernhard Stomporowski, Michael Kobor, Thomas Melges, Kai von Warburg, Uwe Maerz, Michael Buchheit, Olaf Kaska (coxswain)	GER

* In men's lightweight rowing, no rower may weigh over 160 lb.

World Records, women's lightweight* rowing

⏱		🚩
7:24.46	**Single sculls** Zoe McBride	NZL
7:18.32	**Coxless pairs** Eliza Blair, Justine Joyce	AUS
6:47.69	**Double sculls** Maaike Head, Ilse Paulis	NED
6:15.95	**Quad sculls** Mirte Kraaijkamp, Maaike Head Elisabeth Woerner, Ilse Paulis	NED

* In women's lightweight rowing, no rower may weigh over 125 lb.

World Records, indoor* rowing

🏋	🚩	⏱
Open men Josh Dunkley-Smith	AUS	5:35.8
Lightweight men Henrik Stephansen	DEN	5:56.7
Open women Olena Buryak	UKR	6:22.8
Lightweight women Christine Cavallo	USA	6:54.1

* Indoor records are set on a rowing machine.

Team USA women's eight
Between 2006–2017, this squad, which included three of the world's best rowers, went undefeated.

Robbie Manson
When he set his world record, Manson broke the record of fellow New Zealander Mahé Drysdale by three seconds.

Henrik Stephansen
In setting his record, Stephansen became the first 2,000-meter lightweight rower to break six minutes.

Oxford and Cambridge Boat Race

The most famous of all rowing events, the Boat Race between Oxford and Cambridge Universities' crews started in 1829, and has been held annually – more or less – ever since. The women's event began in 1927, was made an annual event in 1964, and was held on The Championship Course for the first time in 2015. This four-mile, side-by-side race is for eight scullers and a female or male cox.

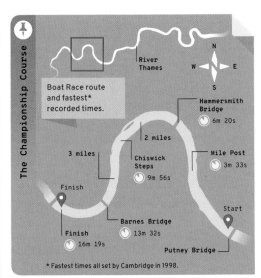

The Championship Course

Boat Race route and fastest* recorded times.

River Thames

N / W / E / S

Hammersmith Bridge — 6m 20s
2 miles
Mile Post — 3m 33s
3 miles
Chiswick Steps — 9m 56s
Finish
Start
Barnes Bridge — 13m 32s
Finish — 16m 19s
Putney Bridge

* Fastest times all set by Cambridge in 1998.

The men's record for the Boat Race is 16 minutes 19 seconds (Cambridge 1998); the women's record is 18 minutes 33 seconds (Cambridge 2017).

List of Boat Race results

	Cambridge (light blue) wins	Oxford (dark blue) wins
Men		
1829–1859	9	7
1860–1889	13	16
1890–1919	9	16
1920–1949	20	4
1950–1979	17	13
1980–2009	11	19
2010–2018	4	5
	83	**80**
Women		
1927–1959	8	10
1960–1989	20	6
1990–2018	15	14
	43	**30**

In 1877 the race was a dead heat (see below left), and there were no races during the World Wars (1915–1919/1940–1945). In 1912 both boats filled with water and the race was stopped.

Factfile

Reserves save the day
Oxford v. Cambridge

When an American was dropped from the Oxford squad weeks before the 1987 race, his American colleagues quit in protest and Oxford reserves were brought in. Though considered the favorite, Cambridge lost by four boat lengths to the less-experienced Oxford team.

Stephen Hawking

Nobel Prize-winning physicist Stephen Hawking (1942–2018) was a cox at Oxford University. Though he never participated in the Boat Race, he was a daredevil cox, steering his boat through the smallest of gaps.

A Moment in Time

Stopped for a duck

Henry Pearce

August 1928

Sloten Canal, Amsterdam

Single sculls quarter final, Olympic Games

Australian rower Henry Pearce had proven himself in the heats, beating opponents by a good margin, and once even waiting on the finish line for his opponent. In the quarter final, Pearce stopped rowing mid-race to let a duck and ducklings pass – he still went on to win the race and the gold!

Controversy

The dead heat

Oxford v. Cambridge

March 24, 1877

The Championship Course

34th Boat Race

There has only ever been one tied Boat Race. Though declared a dead heat, Oxford believed they were the victors. The controversy resulted in finishing posts being installed – they are still in place on the River Thames. Another change was to use umpires representing both universities.

Para Rowing

Athletes with physical or visual impairments are eligible to enter para rowing events at the Paralympics, World Rowing and World Championships (at these last two, para rowers participate alongside able-bodied rowers in some classes). Races of 1,000 meters (2,000 meters for World Rowing) on flat water include single and double sculls and mixed coxed fours.

Paralympic team event gold medalists

	●	●	○	
Men's single sculls				
Ukraine	1	1	0	2
GBR	1	0	1	2
China	1	0	0	1
Women's single sculls				
GBR	2	0	0	2
Ukraine	1	0	0	1
Mixed double sculls				
China	2	1	0	3
GBR	1	0	0	1
Mixed coxed four				
GBR	2	0	1	3
Italy	1	0	0	1

Top medalists, by gold

	●	●	○	
GBR	6	0	2	8
China	3	2	0	5
Ukraine	2	1	1	4

Superstar

Oksana Masters

This Ukraine-born athlete made her mark not just on para rowing winning gold in double sculls in London 2012, but in Paralympic cycling, cross-country skiing and biathlon. Masters was born with radiation-induced birth defects and had both legs amputated above the knee.

2008–   USA

Para Athletes

CANOEING

The events for canoe and kayak races are similar – sprint, slalom, marathon, polo, wildwater and ocean, though only sprint and slalom are at the Olympics. In canoeing, the paddler kneels and uses a single-bladed paddle. In kayaking, the paddler sits and uses an oar with a blade at each end. There are events for individuals and teams. Sprint distances are 200, 500 and 1,000 meters, and over the 200-meter course of a whitewater slalom race there are 18–25 gates to steer between. Marathon races can cover 125 miles, and canoe polo is water polo but in canoes. All canoe and kayak sports demand explosive power, speed, endurance and precision.

> "It takes a lot of hard training, it takes physical ability. Paddling takes technical perfection."
>
> Carrie Johnson, Olympic sprint canoer (2004)

All-Stars

Gert Fredriksson

🕙 c.1948–1960   🏳 Sweden

The most-medaled canoeist, this Swedish sprinter won eight Olympic golds, seven World Championships and 71 national medals. In 1956, the IOC named him the No. 1 sportsman in the world – the only canoeist to have ever been so honored.

Jessica Fox

🕙 2009–   🏳 Australia

In canoe and kayak singles, and teams slalom, Australian Fox has so far accumulated 30 Olympic, Oceania and World Championship medals, along with the 2017 Canoeist of the Year and 2018 World Paddle Sportswoman of the Year awards.

Katalin Kovács

🕙 1987–2013   🏳 Hungary

This Hungarian sprint canoer's trophy cupboard contains eight Olympic, 40 World Championship and 29 European Championship medals – most of them golds. Kovacs has also won Hungarian Sportswoman of the Year three times!

▼ Canoe Sprint World Championships   `ICF`

This international event, hosted by the International Canoe Federation (ICF), is held annually save for Summer Olympic years. There are events for one, two or four rowers in open canoes using a single-bladed paddle, and in kayaks (closed canoes) using a double-bladed paddle. Race distances range from 200–5,000 meters. Paracanoe sprint races – the first ICF Paracanoe was in 2009 – run over a 200-meter course.

Overall top medalists*, by team

🏴	🔴	🔴	🔴	⚪
Hungary	205	153	136	494
Germany	121	91	72	284
Soviet Union URS	102	80	66	248
East Germany GDR	73	36	36	145
Romania	52	76	67	195
Russia	49	49	43	141
Poland	32	74	70	176
Sweden	31	38	44	113
Canada	30	21	23	74
Belarus	19	27	29	75

* Includes all discontinued and current men's and women's events.

Since 2010, there has been a paracanoe sprint championship. It became a Paralympic event in 2016, with six categories for men and women.

Factfile

Hungary

Hungarian canoe sprint teams have dominated this sport, winning 194 world titles (nearly double their nearest rival, Germany) and 77 Olympic medals. But oddly, none of the sport's greatest *individual* athletes are Hungarian.

Champions humbled
Hungary/Germany v. Belarus

The giants of canoe sprint, Hungary and Germany, were humbled at the 2015 World Championships when Belarus topped the gold medal tally. Maryna Litvinchuk (BEL) was the only athlete to win three gold medals at this championships.

▼ Canoe Slalom World Championships   `ICF`

This is also organized by the ICF and runs on a similar schedule to canoe sprint. Once known as whitewater slalom, it requires competitors to turn rapidly in eddies, fast water and even upstream. A slalom course can be completed in 80–120 seconds, and there are time penalties if the kayak or canoe, paddle or athlete touches a pole. There are individual, tandem and team events. France tops the medal table as of 2017.

Top five medalists, by gold*

👤	🏳	🔴	🔴	🔴	⚪
Men					
Michal Martikán	SVK	13	3	5	21
Jon Lugbill	USA	12	1	0	13
Richard Fox	GBR	10	0	1	11
David Hearn	USA	8	5	0	13
Alexander Slafkovský	SVK	8	2	0	10
Women					
Myriam Fox-Jerusalmi	FRA	8	2	0	10
Štěpánka Hilgertová	TCH CZE	7	5	2	14
Jessica Fox	AUS	7	1	2	10
Ludmila Polesná	TCH	4	5	2	11
Ursula Gläser	GDR	4	1	0	5

* Medals won includes individual and team events.

The poles on the slalom course are colored red or green. Canoers paddle upstream – against the current – to negotiate red poles.

Factfile

Michal Martikán

This great Slovakian slalom canoeist competed in five Olympics, winning five medals. He was the youngest-ever winner of a World Cup slalom at the age of 16. His World Championship tally is 21, but Martikán continues to compete and win.

Štěpánka Hilgertová

Known as the "World Slalom's Lady of the Gates," Hilgertová has been on her national Czech team 30 times and competed in six Olympics. Her Olympic and World Championship tally is nine gold medals. She won the World Cup twice.

SAILING

Competitive sailing is a complex sport, divided into many categories based on the type of craft. In the Olympics, there are dinghy (six types including Finns and Lasers), multihull and sailboard events. In other international events there are many more categories, including para sailing. Boats have one or two crew, and there are races for men, women and mixed crews. Competitors in equally matched boats set off at the same time to race the course. The winners are those who have read and mastered the day's wind and sea conditions the best. The crew on these racing boats have stamina, technical ability, competitive drive and a passion for the sport.

> "You haven't won the race, if in winning the race you have lost the respect of your competitors."
>
> Paul Elvstrom, four-time Olympic sailing champion (1948, 1952, 1956, 1960)

All-Stars

Ben Ainslie

1989–   GBR

This British Laser and Finn sailor has four Olympic golds. He also has 12 World Championship titles. With Team Oracle USA, he won the America's Cup in 2013. He now runs his own America's Cup team, BAR, from Portsmouth, UK.

Sarah Ayton

1998–2010   GBR

With one Olympic gold as a single-handed sailor in 2004, Ayton earned her second in 2008 in the world-ranked No. 1 "Three blondes in a boat" team. An Extreme Sailing Series champion, she won Sailor of the Year in 2016.

Bjorn Dunderbeck

1986–   Netherlands

This Dutch windsurfer has won 105 professional windsurfing titles and been awarded Overall World Champion 41 times. This talented and determined athlete broke the nautical mile windsurfing speed record three times.

Focus on the Olympics

Sailing has been an Olympic sport since 1896, but the actual races that year were canceled due to excessive wind. Sailboard (windsurfing) events started in 1984, and they may be joined by a kitesurfing program. The United Kingdom dominates the sailing gold medal table with 28 (to 2016), followed by the USA with 19.

Top medalists*

Men's 470 – two-person dinghy							
Malcolm Page	AUS	1993–	2004, 2008, 2012		2	0	0	2
Women's 470 – two-person dinghy							
Theresa Zabell	ESP	1992–1996	1992, 1996		2	0	0	2
Men's 49er skiff – two-handed high performance dinghy							
Nathan Outteridge	AUS	2002–	2008, 2012	1	1	0	2
Iain Jensen	AUS	2009–	2012	1	1	0	2
Blair Tuke	AUS	2006–	2012	1	1	0	2
Peter Burling	AUS	2009–	2008, 2012	1	1	0	2
Women's 49erFX* – two-handed high performance dinghy							
Kahena Kunze	BRA	2010–	2016	1	0	0	1
Martine Grael	BRA	2009–	2016	1	0	0	1
Finn – one-person dinghy (heavyweight)							
Paul Elvstrøm	DEN	1948–1985	1948, 1952, 1956, 1960, 1968, 1972, 1984, 1988	3	0	0	3
Men's Laser – one-person dinghy							
Tom Burton	AUS	2011–	2016	1	0	0	1
Tom Slingsby	AUS	2007–	2008, 2012	1	0	0	1
Paul Goodison	GBR	2000–	2004, 2008, 2012	1	0	0	1
Women's Laser Radial – one-person dinghy							
Marit Bouwmeester	NED	2010–	2012, 2016	1	1	0	2
Men's RS:X – windsurfing (sailboarding)							
Dorian van Rijsselberge	NED	2001–	2012	2	0	0	2
Women's RS:X – windsurfing (sailboarding)							
Charline Picon	FRA	2009–	2012, 2016	1	0	0	1
Marina Alabau Neira	ESP	2004–	2008, 2012, 2016	1	0	0	1
Jian Yin	CHN	2004–	2004, 2008	1	0	0	1
Mixed Nacra 17* – two-handed mixed crew multihull							
Santiago Lange	ARG	1985–	1988, 1996, 2000, 2004, 2008, 2016	1	0	0	1
Cecilia Carranza Saroli	ARG	2004–	2008, 2012, 2016	1	0	0	1

* Highest medal winners for all 10 current Olympic sailing events. Nacra 17 and 49erFX were new classes for 2016.

Factfile

Tactical brilliance
Ben Ainslie v. Robert Scheidt

In the Laser finals at the 2000 Olympics, GBR's Ainslie had to beat Brazilian Scheidt. Tactical moves before the start gave Ainslie his break, and it was a duel (with fouls and collisions) down Sydney Harbour. Scheidt almost did enough, but Ainslie won the gold!

Twenty-year rivalry
Alessandra Sensini v. Barbara Kendall

These two women – one from Italy, the other from New Zealand – top the medal tally (three) in windsurfing. These rivals faced each other in four Olympics (1996, 2000, 2004, 2008), and between them medaled 19 times on Mistrals and RS:Xs in World Championships.

Canoeing   Sailing

ALPINE SKIING

Alpine skiing is a winter sport that takes place on snow-covered slopes. Unlike Nordic skiing, alpine is a downhill event, with the skier's feet fully clipped into the ski bindings. The skier uses poles for rhythm and balance, especially in the turns. Helmets have to be worn in competition. There are four alpine disciplines: downhill, super-giant (super-G) slalom, slalom and giant slalom. Downhill and super-G are about speed, slalom and giant slalom about clean turns between gates. Super-G is the fastest slalom race, but downhill racers can hit speeds of 99 mph! Combined events consist of one downhill and one or two slalom races.

> "I want to keep pushing the limits... That's the nice thing about ski racing – no one is stopping you from going faster."
>
> Lindsey Vonn, champion alpine skier

All-Stars

Ingemar Stenmark

1973–1989   Sweden

Alongside his three Olympic and five World Championship medals for Sweden, Stenmark had 86 wins in 16 seasons in the World Cup. In this competition, skiers compete in downhill, slalom, giant slalom, super-G and a combined event.

Lindsey Vonn

2001–   USA

The most successful female skier to date, Vonn has three Olympic and seven World Championship medals, plus 82 World Cup wins. This American athlete has been Sportswoman of the Year and has been on the podium in every alpine skiing discipline.

Hermann Maier

1996–2009   Austria

Nicknamed the "Herminator," this Austrian skier has four World Cups, three World Championships and two Olympic golds. Maier is known for his strength – a change from the boy sent home from ski school at 15 for being too small!

Record Breakers

Most race wins at the Alpine World Cup (FIS)

			🏆	DH*	SG*	GS*	SL*	KB*
Men								
Ingemar Stenmark	SWE	1973–1989	86	0	0	46	40	0
Marcel Hirscher	AUT	2007–	56	0	1	28	27	0
Hermann Maier	AUT	1996–2009	54	15	24	14	0	1
Alberto Tomba	ITA	1986–1998	50	0	0	15	35	0
Marc Girardelli	LUX	1980–1996	46	3	9	7	16	11
Pirmin Zurbriggen	SUI	1981–1990	40	10	10	7	2	11
Benjamin Raich	AUT	1996–2015	36	0	1	14	14	7
Aksel Lund Svindal	NOR	2001–	35	14	16	4	0	1
Bode Miller	USA	1997–2017	33	8	5	9	5	6
Stephan Eberharter	AUT	1989–2004	29	18	6	5	0	0
Women								
Lindsey Vonn	USA	2001–	82	43	28	4	2	5
Annemarie Moser-Pröll	AUT	1969–1980	62	36	0	16	3	7
Vreni Schneider	SUI	1984–1995	55	0	0	20	34	1
Renate Götschl	AUT	1993–2009	46	24	17	0	1	4
Anja Pärson	SWE	1998–2012	42	6	4	11	18	3
Mikaela Shiffrin	USA	2012–	40	1	0	6	32	1
Marlies Schild	AUT	2001–2014	37	0	0	1	35	1
Katja Seizinger	GER	1989–1998	36	16	16	4	0	0
Hanni Wenzel	LIE	1972–1984	33	2	0	12	11	8
Erika Hess	SUI	1978–1987	31	0	0	6	21	4

* DH=downhill; SG=super-G; GS=giant slalom; SL=slalom; KB=combined (downhill and one or two slalom runs).

Most World Cups in each discipline

		🏆	
Men			
Ingemar Stenmark	SWE	8	GS
		8	S
Kjetil Andre Aamodt	NOR	5	KB
Hermann Maier	AUT	5	SG
Aksel Lund Svindal	NOR	5	SG
Women			
Lindsey Vonn	USA	8	DH
		5	SG
Katja Seizinger	GER	5	SG

Season prize money at the World Cup

Men		
Marcel Hirscher	AUT	669,681 CHF
Women		
Mikaela Shiffrin	USA	702,774.88 CHF

Prize money earned in Swiss francs (CHF) at 2018 World Cup.

Top recorded speed at the World Cup

Men			
Johan Clarey	2013	FRA	161.9 kph
Women			
Lindsey Vonn	2012	USA	138 kph
Katharina Gutensohn	1990	AUT	138 kph

Age records at the Olympics

Oldest medalist (bronze)			
Bode Miller	USA	2014	36
Oldest gold medalist			
Mario Matt	AUT	2014	34
Youngest medalist (bronze)			
Traudl Hecher	AUT	1960	16
Youngest gold medalist			
Michela Figini	SUI	1984	17

Smallest winning margin* at the Olympics

1994 men's giant slalom

Markus Wasmeier	GER	2.52.46
Urs Kaelin	SUI	2.52.48

Winning margin 0.02 seconds

* Both skiers were competing for gold in the giant slalom, with Wasmeier winning by two milliseconds.

Gold medal sweeps* at the Olympics

Jean-Claude Killy	FRA	1968
Toni Sailer	AUT	1956

* Sweep: when one skier wins gold in every alpine event during one Olympics.

Focus on the Olympics

Alpine ski events for men and women were introduced to the Winter Olympics in 1936 in Germany. Before this, the only Olympic event was Nordic (cross-country) skiing. Super-G – a downhill with wide-set slalom gates – was the most recent addition to the games. Super-G, like downhill, is a speed event while slalom and giant slalom test technical ability.

Gold medal leaders

Men		
Kjetil André Aamodt	NOR	4
Alberto Tomba	ITA	3
Jean-Claude Killy	FRA	3
Toni Sailer	AUT	3
Women		
Janica Kostelić	CRO	4
Maria Höfl-Riesch	GER	3
Deborah Compagnoni	ITA	3
Katja Seizinger	GER	3
Vreni Schneider	SUI	3

Overall gold medal leaders (team)

	●	●	●	○
Austria	37	41	43	121
Switzerland	22	22	22	66
France	15	16	17	48

Factfile

Kjetil André Aamodt

Norway's most decorated ski racer, Aamodt's eight Olympic medals put him at the top of the alpine skiing medal chart. Though an all-around competitor, his three golds came in the super-G.

Austria

Austrians were the first to slide down slopes on wooden planks, then inventing and refining skiing techniques. Austrian slope legends include Hermann Maier, Franz Klammer and Toni Sailer.

Alpine Ski World Cup   [FIS]

The first World Cup was held in 1967, with combined events and super-G added later. Held annually, it ranks second to the Olympics in importance. Austria tops the medal table, followed by Switzerland and the USA. Competitions are most frequently hosted in Europe, Canada and the USA, but are attended by skiers from 115 countries.

Three-plus overall wins*

		🏆
Men		
Marcel Hirscher	AUT	7
Marc Girardelli	LUX	5
Hermann Maier	AUT	4
Pirmin Zurbriggen	SUI	4
Gustav Thöni	ITA	4
Phil Mahre	USA	3
Ingemar Stenmark	SWE	3
Women		
Annemarie Moser-Pröll	AUT	6
Lindsey Vonn	USA	4
Vreni Schneider	SUI	3
Janica Kostelić	CRO	3
Petra Kronberger	AUT	3

* **Overall wins:** skiers with the most points across all events are overall winners. Marcel Hirscher and Mikaela Shiffrin were 2017-2018 overall winners.

Factfile

World Cup Crystal Globe

Weighing 16.3 lb., the lead-crystal Crystal Globe is presented to the skier with the highest points tally at the end of the season. Winners of individual disciplines receive a 7.7 lb. crystal globe.

Marcel Hirscher

This Austrian slalom king started skiing at just 30 months old. He has since won the overall World Cup title seven times in a row (2012–2018), along with three Olympic medals, including two golds.

A Moment in Time

Downhill crash

 Hermann Maier

📅 February 13, 1998

📍 Nagano, Japan

🚩 Downhill race, Winter Olympics

Just a few days before Hermann Maier won gold in the giant slalom and super-G, he crashed in the downhill at 80 mph. He flew 30 feet in the air, landed on his head, flipped a few times and went through the fencing. Maier did not move – the worst was feared – but then he got up and walked away.

Controversy

Mystery man in black

📅 February 17, 1968

📍 Chamrousse, France

🚩 Slalom, Winter Olympics

In thick fog, Austrian Karl Schranz claimed his slalom run had been impeded by a man in black. Officials allowed him a second run, but then disqualified him for missing a gate on his first run. Many believed a French official had crossed Schranz's path to guarantee that French skier, Jean-Claude Killy, would win.

Para Skiing

The current list of alpine ski events for the Paralympic Winter Games includes downhill, slalom, giant slalom, super-G and super combined. Skiers, cutting over the snow at speeds of over 80 mph, can compete standing on one or two skis or seated on a sit-ski. Visually impaired skiers follow their guide and his or her radio instructions. Para alpine skiing entered the Paralympics in 1976.

Individual Paralympic medal leaders

		●	●	●	○
Men					
Gerd Schönfelder	GER	16	4	2	22
Rolf Heinzmann	SUI	12	2	0	14
Martin Braxenthaler	GER	10	1	1	12
Hans Burn	SUI	6	5	3	14
Greg Mannino	USA	6	4	2	12
Bernard Baudean	FRA	6	4	1	11
Michael Milton	AUS	6	3	2	11
Tristan Mouric	FRA	6	3	1	10
Josef Meusburger	AUT	6	2	0	8
Cato Zahl Pedersen	NOR	6	1	0	7
Brian Santos	USA	6	0	0	6
Women					
Reinhild Moeller	FRG GER	16	2	1	19
Sarah Will	USA	12	1	0	13
Lauren Woolstencroft	CAN	8	1	1	10
Sarah Billmeier	USA	7	5	1	13
Nancy Gustafson	USA	7	1	0	8

Superstar

Gerd Schönfelder

The most medaled para alpine skier (22 including 16 golds) in the sport's history also has multiple World Championships and World Cups. At age 19, Schönfelder lost his right arm and four fingers from his left hand. Because of this, he skis without poles.

⏱ 1992–2011   🚩 Germany

 Para Athletes

Alpine skiing

OTHER WINTER SPORTS

There is a wide range of winter sports. Some, like curling, are about accuracy, while speed skating is pure acceleration. Figure skating asks its competitors to be athletes, gymnasts and dancers. Ski jumpers defy gravity, turning their bodies into an airplane wing, then landing gracefully on two skis as far as possible from the 90- or 120-meter-high take-off point. Among the earliest Olympic events were cross-country skiing, bobsleigh, figure and speed skating, and ski jumping. More recent additions include snowboarding (1998), skeleton (2002) and short-track speed skating (1992).

> "Snowboarding is an activity that is very popular with people who do not feel that regular skiing is lethal enough."
>
> Dave Barry, Pulitzer-winning author

All-Stars

Gregor Schlierenzauer

2005–   Austria

This ski jumper has four Olympic medals, 12 World Championships, five ski flying World Championships and a World Cup. In ski flying (ski jumping Nordic style), athletes glide distances 66% longer than in alpine ski jumping.

Marit Bjørgen

1999–2018   Norway

This Norwegian is ranked No. 1, with the most Winter Olympics medals of any athlete contending the World Cup. Bjørgen competed in cross-country skiing across all disciplines and won the International Fair Play award in 2014.

Shaun White

1999–   USA

This American snowboarder has three Olympic halfpipe golds and 18 superpipe and slopestyle Winter X Games medals. He was the first to land back-to-back double corkscrews and holds the highest score in Olympic halfpipe (97.75).

Record Breakers

Longest recorded ski jumps

Men			
Stefan Kraft*	AUT	2017	253.5 m
Women			
Daniela Iraschko	AUT	2003	200.0 m

* Stefan Kraft has jumped over 250 meters three times.

Perfect score* ski jumps

Jurij Tepeš	SLO	2015	244.0 m
Peter Prevc	SLO	2015	233.0 m
Kazuyoshi Funaki	JPN	1998	205.5 m
Kazuyoshi Funaki	JPN	1998	187.5 m
Anton Innauer	AUT	1976	176.0 m
Wolfgang Loitzl	AUT	2009	142.5 m
Sven Hannawald	GER	2003	142.0 m
Hideharu Miyahira	JPN	2003	135.5 m
Kazuyoshi Funaki	JPN	1998	132.5 m
Kazuyoshi Funaki	JPN	1999	119.0 m

* **Perfect score:** when a ski jump receives maximum style points (20) from each of the five judges.

Oldest Winter Olympic gold medalists

Men			
Robin Welsh	GBR	Curling	54
Women			
Anette Norberg	SWE	Curling	43

Youngest Winter Olympic gold medalists

Men			
Toni Nieminen	FIN	Ski jumping	16
Women			
Kim Yun-Mi	KOR	Short-track speed skating	13

Oldest Winter Olympic competitors

Men			
Carl August Kronlund	SWE	Curling	58
Women			
Cheryl Bernard	CAN	Curling	51

Youngest Winter Olympic competitors

Men			
Alain Giletti	FRA	Figure skating	12
Women			
Cecilia Colledge	GBR	Figure skating	11

Absolute best total scores* figure skating

Men		
Yuzuru Hanyu	JPN	330.43
Women		
Evgenia Medvedeva	RUS	241.31
Pairs		
Aliona Savchenko Bruno Massot	GER	245.84
Ice dance pairs		
Gabriella Papadakis Guillaume Cizeron	FRA	207.20

* **Total score:** all points earned by a skater in his or her short and free program.

World records in long track* speed skating

Men			
Pavel Kulizhnikov	RUS	500 m	33.98
Shani Davis	USA	1,000 m	1:06.42
Denis Yuskov	RUS	1,500 m	1:41.02
Ted-Jan Bloemen	CAN	5,000 m	6:01.86
Ted-Jan Bloemen	CAN	10,000 m	12:36.30
Women			
Lee Sang-hwa	KOR	500 m	36.36
Nao Kodaira	JPN	1,000 m	1:12.09
Heather Richardson-Bergsma	USA	1,500 m	1:50.85
Cindy Klassen	CAN	3,000 m	3:53.34
Martina Sáblíková	CZE	5,000 m	6:42.66

* This takes place on a 400-meter oval track. Long track speed skating started in 1892.

World records in short track* speed skating

Men			
Wu Dajing	CHN	500 m	39.584
Hwang Dae-heon	KOR	1,000 m	1:20.875
Sjinkie Knegt	NED	1,500 m	2:07.943
Women			
Elise Christie	GBR	500 m	42.335
Shim Suk-hee	KOR	1,000 m	1:26.661
Choi Min-jeong	KOR	1,500 m	2:14.354

* This takes place on a 111.12-meter oval track.

Marathon ice speed world hour record*

Men		
Erik Jan Kooiman	NED	43,735.94 m
Women		
Carien Kleibeuker	NED	40,569.56 m

* These unofficial records (not recognized by ISU) are for distance speed skated in one hour on an indoor oval track. Both records were set in 2015.

Focus on the Olympics

Alpine skiing and ice hockey are premier draws at the Winter Olympics, but the remaining 13 events also attract huge numbers of viewers and astounding athletes. Curling, where the distance and direction of stones is controlled by sweeping the ice, has become hotly contended. Skeleton racers, who steer headfirst down a treacherous steep ice slope, reach speeds of over 80 mph.

Most successful medalists*, men

		●	●	○	
⚲ Biathlon					
Ole Einar Bjørndalen	NOR	8	4	1	13
Ricco Groß	GER	4	3	1	8
Emil Hegle Svendsen	NOR	4	3	1	8
Sven Fischer	GER	4	2	2	8
⚲ Cross-country					
Bjørn Dæhlie	NOR	8	4	0	12
Sixten Jernberg	SWE	4	3	2	9
⚲ Speed skating					
Sven Kramer	NED	4	2	3	9
⚲ Short track speed skating					
Viktor Ahn	KOR RUS	6	0	2	8
Apolo Anton Ohno	USA	2	2	4	8

Most successful medalists*, women

		●	●	○	
⚲ Biathlon					
Uschi Disl	GER	2	4	3	9
⚲ Cross-country					
Marit Bjørgen	NOR	8	4	3	15
Raisa Smetanina	URS/EUN	4	5	1	10
Stefania Belmondo	ITA	2	3	5	10
Lyubov Yegorova	EUN/RUS	6	3	0	9
Charlotte Kalla	SWE	3	6	0	9
Galina Kulakova	URS	4	2	2	8
⚲ Speed skating					
Ireen Wüst	NED	5	5	1	11
Claudia Pechstein	GER	5	2	2	9
Karin Enke	GDR	3	4	1	8
Gunda Niemann-Stirnemann	GER	3	4	1	8
⚲ Short track speed skating					
Arianna Fontana	ITA	1	2	5	8

*Men and women who have won at least eight medals, excluding alpine skiing (*see pp 48–49*) and ice hockey (*see pp 36–37*).

Sporting Arenas

M-Wave
Built for the 1998 Winter Olympics speed skating events, and named for the M-shaped sections of its roof, the M-wave continues to be the site of record attempts.

👥 18,000   🎿 1996   📍 Nagano, Japan

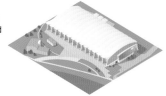

Richmond Olympic Oval
Used as the 2010 speed skating venue, its roof design is inspired by the wings of a heron. The building's *feng shui* was considered during planning.

👥 8,000   🎿 2008   📍 Richmond, British Columbia, Canada

Fisht (Olympic) Stadium
The roof, made of almost 40,000 yards of a plastic polymer, resembles snowy peaks. Originally enclosed, it is now open-air, and home to the Russian national football team. It was a 2018 World Cup venue.

👥 40,000   🎿 2013   📍 Sochi, Russia

A Moment in Time

Bobsleigh's coolest underdogs

🏳 Jamaica

📅 February 1988

📍 Calgary, Alberta, Canada

🏹 Four-man bobsleigh, Winter Olympics 1988

Even though they crashed out during a qualifier, Devon Harris, Dudley Stokes, Michael White, Freddy Powell and Chris Stokes caught the world's imagination, their story told in the film *Cool Runnings*. Even with little real track time and borrowed equipment, they were the "hottest thing on ice."

Controversy

Figure skater attacked

👤 Nancy Kerrigan

📅 January 6, 1994

📍 Cobo Arena, Detroit, Michigan

🏹 US Figure Skating Championships

In the lead-up to the 1994 Winter Olympics, US figure skater Nancy Kerrigan was attacked with a metal rod, in order to end her Olympic dream and give Sonya Harding a chance. (The failed attack was planned by Harding's ex-husband.) At the Olympics, Harding came eighth and Kerrigan won silver.

Paralympic Winter Sports

Current events for the Paralympic Winter Games (save alpine skiing and ice hockey) include biathlon, cross country skiing, ice-sledge speed racing, snowboarding and wheelchair curling. Bobsleigh will be added in 2022. Curlers use wheelchairs and can release the stone by hand or with a stick. Snowboarders have equipment modified for their needs.

Athletes with most Paralympic medals

		●	●	●	○	
⚲ Biathlon						
Verena Bentele	GER	3	0	1	4	
Frank Höfle	GER	3	0	1	4	
Wilhelm Brem	GER	2	1	1	4	
Anne Floriet	FRA	1	2	1	4	
⚲ Cross-country skiing						
Frank Höfl	GER FRG	10	5	2	17	
⚲ Snowboarding						
Bibian Mentel-Spee*	NED	3	0	0	3	
⚲ Wheelchair curling						
Sonja Gaudet	CAN	3	0	0	3	
Jalle Jungnell	SWE	0	0	2	2	
⚲ Ice-sledge speed racing						
Knut Lundstrøm	NOR	8	3	1	12	

*Within four months of a leg amputation, Mentel-Spee was snowboarding, but couldn't yet walk with crutches.

Superstar ⭐

Ragnhild Myklebust

In every Paralympic event she entered, Myklebust won a medal! Her medal total from five Paralympics was 27, including 22 golds. She was also undefeated in cross country. She suffers from polio and uses a sit-ski or mono-ski and lightweight ice sledge.

🕐 1988–2002   🏳 Norway

Para Athletes

Other Winter sports

RUGBY

There are two codes of rugby: union and league. They are both contact sports, using an egg-shaped ball that can be moved forward by kicking or running with it (passing may only go backward). Points are scored with tries (grounding the ball behind the try line) and kicking the ball between the posts. A game is two halves of 40 minutes, and the player with the ball can be tackled. While a union team has 15 on-field players, a league team has 13. In union there are more opportunities to regain possession of the ball than in league, and when the ball goes into touch in union there is a line-out; in league, a scrum. Both are hard and physically demanding sports.

> "Remember that rugby is a team game; all 14 of you make sure you pass the ball to Jonah [Lomu]."
> Anonymous fax to the New Zealand All Blacks (rugby union) before the 1995 World Cup semifinal against England

All-Stars

Dan Carter
🔍 2003–   🏳️ New Zealand

The greatest rugby union fly half ever, this New Zealand All Black is the highest point scorer in Test and Super Rugby, and was named International Player of the Year three times for his mastery of every aspect of the game.

Brian O'Driscoll
🔍 1996–2014   🏳️ Ireland

The talent of this outside center Irish player was evident when he scored a hat trick for Ireland in France in 2000. He is the most capped player in rugby union history, and the highest try scorer in Irish rugby.

David Campese
🔍 1982–1996   🏳️ Australia

This union winger ranks third on the most tries scored (64) in Test matches. He played 67 winning Tests for the Australian Wallabies. His unique goose-step left opponents wondering which way he went!

Rugby World Cup

The Webb Ellis Cup trophy (named for the Rugby School pupil rumored to have invented rugby) is presented to the winners of this international tournament. It is held every four years – the first men's World Cup was in 1987 – and currently 20 nations compete over a six-week period for a place in the final. The women's World Cup began in 1991 and 12 countries compete. New Zealand tops both World Cups.

Results

	🏆	🥈	score
Men			
1987	New Zealand	France	29–9
1991	Australia	England	12–6
1995	South Africa	New Zealand	15–12
1999	Australia	France	35–12
2003	England	Australia	20–17
2007	South Africa	England	15–6
2011	New Zealand	France	8–7
2015	New Zealand	Australia	34–17
Women			
1991	USA	England	19–6
1994	England	USA	38–23
1998	New Zealand	USA	44–12
2002	New Zealand	England	19–9
2006	New Zealand	England	25–17
2010	New Zealand	England	13–10
2014	England	Canada	21–9
2017	New Zealand	England	41–32

Factfile

New Zealand
The All Blacks have won three World Cups and 75% of all matches they have played in their 125-year history. They are known for their fearsome "No excuses" play, and the traditional Māori *haka* war dance they perform before all matches.

Jonah Lomu
Regarded as the finest rugby player ever, this All Blacks winger played 63 Tests, scoring 37 tries between 1994–2002, but it was his run past several English players in the 1995 World Cup that made his reputation. Lomu died in 2015, age 40.

WORLD RUGBY

Rugby League World Cup

RLIF

There have been 15 Rugby League World Cup men's tournaments since the first in 1954. It is now held regularly every four years with some 19 national teams from North America, Europe, Asia-Pacific and South Africa taking part. Australia, France and New Zealand have played in every tournament. A women's World Cup started in 2000, and eight national teams compete. New Zealand has won this tournament three times.

Succesful nations

	🏆	🥈	📅
Men			
Australia	11	3	2017
Great Britain*	3	4	1972
New Zealand	1	3	2008
England	0	3	
France	0	2	
Women			
New Zealand	3	2	2008
Australia	2	1	2017
Great Britain*	0	1	
New Zealand	0	1	

* GB men's team once represented England, Scotland and Wales, but from 1995 three separate teams compete. GB women's team represents England, Scotland and Wales.

> In the 2005 women's World Cup final, New Zealand defeated the New Zealand Maori team 58–0. In the next tournament final, Australia beat New Zealand 34–0.

Factfile

Australia
The Kangaroos have won 11 of the 15 World Cups and been runners-up three times. Their greatest winning margin of 106 points was against Russia in 2000. Players for the national squad are usually drawn from NRL (National Rugby League) teams.

Darren Lockyer
As fullback and then five-eighth, Lockyer played nine World Cup matches scoring five tries and four goals. He was Kangaroo captain 2003–2011 and won the Golden Boot Award twice. His club team was the Brisbane Broncos of Queensland.

CRICKET

Cricket is played by two teams of 11 players. While one team bats, the other bowls and fields. The batting team aims to score runs while the bowling team tries to limit them. When a bowled ball is hit, the two batsmen/women run between two wickets (three stumps topped by two bails). One run earns one point; a boundary, four; and a ball that clears the field, six. There are several ways for a batter to be out, including if the ball is caught, hits the wicket or is blocked from hitting the wicket. When the batting team is out, they bowl and field. The quickest game (Twenty20) lasts around four hours, and the longest (men's Test cricket), five days. The women's game follows the Laws of Cricket but with a few variations.

> "They came to see me bat not you bowl."
>
> WG Grace, English cricket legend (1865–1908) to the bowler on Grace being bowled out on the first ball

All-Stars

Sachin Tendulkar

🔄 1989–2013   🏳 India

This legendary Indian batsman was the first to score 100 centuries (100 runs in an innings) in international Tests, and the first to score 200-plus runs in a One Day International (ODI). His career tally of 15,921 runs remains unbeaten.

Sydney Barnes

🔄 1894–1930   🏳 ENG

A fast–medium and leg spin bowler who was always on length and accurate, Barnes' 1913–1914 record of 49 wickets, including 17 wickets for 159 runs, still stands. He remains No. 1 on the International Cricket Council (ICC) rankings of bowlers.

Garfield Sobers

🔄 1954–1974   🏳 West Indes

Sobers could bat, bowl and field. He was a leading run-scorer (once hitting six sixes in an over), the greatest stroke-player, second-highest wicket-taker for the West Indies and No. 3 on all-time catches taken in the field.

▼ The Ashes   `ICC`

A Test match is any played between 12 national men's teams, but a Test series between Australia and England is called The Ashes. The rivalry between the teams is fierce, with national honor at stake. An Ashes tour consists of five Tests, each lasting around five days, and is played every two years in either Australia or England. The winner claims The Ashes replica. The original urn is at Lord's Cricket Ground, London.

The Ashes tour records to 2017–2018

🏳	🏆
Number of Ashes tour wins (70 tours played with 5 draws)	
Australia	33
England	32
Number of Test match wins (330 matches played with 90 draws)	
Australia	134
England	106

The Ashes win and loss margins

🏳	▤
Narrowest winning margin	
England (2005)	2 runs
Largest winning margin	
England (1928)	675 runs
Number of centuries* scored	
Australia	264
England	212

* Century: 100 runs by one batter in one innings.

Factfile

The Ashes urn

This modest six-inch-tall terracotta urn supposedly contains the ashes of a wooden cricket bail that was burned after England lost the 1882 Test against Australia. The ashes marked the "death of English cricket."

The Bodyline Tour (1932–1933)
Australia v. England

In this Ashes tour, English bowlers pitched the ball so it reared up dangerously at the batsman's body. Bodyline bowling was not illegal, just unsporting. England won this tour, but bodyline (later banned) soured relations between the two countries.

▼ Cricket World Cup   `ICC`

Held every four years, it is the championship for men's and women's One Day International (ODI) cricket. In the ODI game, bowling overs are limited to 50 with six balls per over. (There is no overs limit in Test cricket.) A match lasts one day (including floodlit day–night matches), each team plays one batting and one bowling innings, player uniforms are in national colors and the ball is white or pink.

Winners and runners-up in the World Cup

🏳	🏆	2	📅★
Men			
Australia	5	2	2015
India	2	1	2011
West Indies	2	1	1979
Sri Lanka	1	2	1996
Pakistan	1	1	1992
England	0	3	
New Zealand	0	1	
Women			
Australia	6	2	2013
England	4	3	2017
New Zealand	1	3	2000
India	0	2	
West Indies	0	1	

The closest World Cup final (1987) was won by just seven runs! England just couldn't muster any more to prevent the first of Australia's World Cup trophies.

Factfile

Australia

Between 1999–2007 Australia dominated ODI cricket, including a 32-week winning streak and three ICC World Cups. The killer teams included Glenn McGrath, Ricky Ponting, Shane Warne, Matthew Hayden, Steve Waugh and Adam Gilchrist.

"David v. Goliath"
West Indies v. India

The mighty West Indies was expected to win the 1983 final against first-time finalists India. Though faced with bowlers Joel Garner and Michael Holding, the Indians got 183 runs, and then nailed the West Indies' batsmen all-out for 140 runs.

HORSE RACING

Record Breakers

This ancient sport has changed little over time. The aim has always been to discover which horse could cover a course in the shortest time. There are several types of horse racing around the world, including steeplechase, jump, harness and endurance. Thoroughbred flat racing is the most popular in the US and is held on a level track, up to 1.5 miles long. The Melbourne Cup, Kentucky Derby and Epsom Derby are famous thoroughbred racing events. In jump racing, horse and jockey have to clear a series of fences on a longer course. While all horses can gallop, very few have the build, stamina and intelligence to be a successful racehorse.

> "There is no place for arrogance or complacency in racing because you are up there one minute and on your backside the next."
>
> AP McCoy, Champion Jockey (1995–2015)

All-Stars

Russell Baze

🔄 1974–2016   🏳 USA/Canada

Baze won 12,842 races in 53,578 starts – a standing North American record – and had a win percentage of 24! This Canadian-American is the only jockey to win 400 or more races in seven consecutive years.

Frankie Dettori

🔄 1986–   🏳 Italy

One of this Italian jockey's most celebrated moments was riding all seven winners on British Champions' Day at Ascot in 1996. Named Champion Jockey three times, he was a teenager when he rode his first 100 winners in one season.

AP "Tony" McCoy

🔄 1992–2015   🏳 GBR

McCoy had 4,358 winners in jump racing and was Champion Jockey 20 times. The Irish rider won every big race possible including the Cheltenham Gold Cup, Champion Hurdle, King George VI Chase and the Grand National.

Top-rated flat racers* (3+ years old)

🐎	⚔	🏆	🔄
Frankel	14	14	2010–2012
Sea Bird	8	7	1964–1965
Brigadier Gerard	18	17	1970–1972
Tudor Minstrel	10	8	1946–1947
Abernant	17	14	1948–1950
Ribot	16	16	1954–1956
Mill Reef	14	12	1970–1972
Dancing Brave	10	8	1985–1986
Dubai Millennium	10	9	1998–2000

* Flat racers: mounted horses that run on a level racetrack over certain distances.

Top-rated jump chasers*

🐎	⚔	🏆	🔄
Arkle	26	22	1962–1966
Sprinter Sacre	18	14	2007–2016
Kauto Star	31	19	2004–2012
Mill House	34	16	c.1963–1968
Desert Orchid	23	13	1983–1991
Dunkirk	3	0	2009
Burrough Hill Lad	27	17	1982–1988
Moscow Flyer	45	27	2000–2006
Long Run	34	15	2010–2016
Denman	19	10	2005–2011

* Jump chasers: mounted horses that run in steeplechases, which is a race run over fences.

The greatest trainers

👤	🏳	🔄	🏆
Bob Baffert	USA	1973–	2,800+
Todd Pletcher	USA	1995–	4,000+
Henry Cecil	GBR	1969–2013	-
Aidan O'Brien	IRE	1994–	-
D Wayne Lukas	USA	1968–	4,741+
William I Mott	USA	1978–	3,780+
Steve Asmussen	USA	1986–	7,823+
Bart Cummings	AUS	1953–2015	1,041
Vincent O'Brien	IRE	c.1948–1994	-
Luca Cumani	ITA	1976–	-

$10-million prize winning horses

🐎	🏳	💰
Orfevre	JPN	$19,005,276
Gentildonna	JPN	$18,468,392
Arrogate	USA	$17,422,600
Buena Vista	JPN	$17,018,548
Kitasan Black	JPN	$16,572,523
T M Opera O	JPN	$16,200,337
Gun Runner	USA	$15,988,500
Winx	AUS	$15,500,000
Gold Ship	JPN	$15,040,217
California Chrome	USA	$14,752,650

💰 These horses earned their prize money mostly racing in Japan, Hong Kong, Australia and Dubai.

Top-rated jump hurdlers*

🐎	⚔	🏆	🔄
Night Nurse	-	19	1973–1981
Istabraq	29	23	1997–2002
Monksfield	-	6	c.1978–1980
Persian War	51	18	1966–1973
Comedy of Errors	48	23	c.1971–1976
Le Sauvignon	16	11	c.1997–2002
Lanzarote	33	20	-
Limestone Lad	47	29	1997–2003
Bird's Nest	62	19	c.1975–1980

* Jump hurdlers: mounted horses that jump hurdles placed on a level course. Some information for this list unavailable.

Top-rated harness racers*

🐎	⚔	🏆	🔄
Blacks A Fake	105	72	2003–2011
Popular Alm	62	49	1980–1984
Village Kid	160	93	1985–1993
Westburn Grant	67	38	1987–1993
Preux Chevalier	56	41	1982–1986
Gammalite	179	94	1978–1985
Im Themightyquinn	111	58	2006–2015
Our Sir Vancelot	97	48	1995–1999
Smoken Up	153	74	2004–2014
Pure Steel	127	68	1973–1982

* Harness racers: these horses race at a trot or pace while pulling a two-wheeled cart (sulky) in which the jockey sits.

North American fastest time records

⏩	🐎	⏱
Dirt* course		
Two furlongs	Winning Brew	0:20.57
Four furlongs	Oklahoma Natural	0:43.20
Six furlongs	Twin Sparks	1:06.49
One mile	Dr. Fager	1:32.20
One and one half miles	Secretariat	2:24.00
Two miles	Kelso	3:19.20
Turf (grass)* course		
Five furlongs	Pay Any Price	0:53.61
One mile	Mandurah	1:31.23
One and one quarter miles	Red Giant	1:57.16
One and one half miles	Twilight Eclipse	2:22.63
One and three quarter miles	Inaugural Address	2:53.35
All-weather* course		
Five furlongs	M One Rifle	0:55.98
One mile	El Gato Malo	1:33.37
One and one half miles	Muhannak	2:28.24

* Dirt tracks are the fastest racing surface when they are firm. Hard turf surfaces suit high speed thoroughbred racing, but soft turf is better for jump racing. All-weather tracks are made of man-made synthetics to look like turf or dirt tracks.

EQUESTRIAN SPORTS

This sport is all about rider and horse working together to execute complicated moves (dressage), astounding jumps (show jumping over fences, walls, bars and water) and feats of stamina and athleticism (eventing, endurance, carriage driving and vaulting). There are also competitions in Western riding (reining), tent pegging and horseball. Olympic equestrian events for able-bodied athletes started in 1900, and in 1996 for para athletes. Saddles for para riders are made with extra padding, and for the safety of both horse and rider, tack and equipment use Velcro and rubber bands that break away during a fall.

"All equestrians, if they last long enough, learn that riding in whatever form is a lifelong sport and art..."

Jane Smiley, Pulitzer Prize-winning author

Focus on the Olympics

Until 1948, only commissioned military officers and men of stature could compete. In 1952 the field was opened to all comers, though women could initially only enter dressage events. Though the rules have changed, the program – individual and team eventing, show jumping and dressage – has remained basically unchanged since 1912. It is the only Olympic sport where men and women compete against each other.

Winners of five-plus Olympic medals*

		●	●	●	○
Isabell Werth	GER	6	4	0	10
Reiner Klimke	GER	6	0	2	8
Hans Günter Winkler	GER	5	1	1	7
Charles Pahud de Mortanges	NED	4	1	0	5
Anky van Grunsven	NED	3	5	1	9
Michael Plumb	USA	2	4	0	6
Earl Foster Thomson	USA	2	3	0	5
Josef Neckermann	GER	2	2	2	6
André Jousseaume	FRA	2	2	1	5
Liselott Linsenhoff	GER	2	2	1	5
Mark Todd	NZL	2	1	3	6
Christine Stückelberger	SUI	1	3	1	5
Raimondo D'Inzeo	ITA	1	2	3	6
Henri Chammartin	SUI	1	2	2	5
Gustav Fischer	SUI	0	3	2	5
Piero D'Inzeo	ITA	0	2	4	6

* Includes all individual and team events.

Factfile

Germany

The national team of Germany tops the Olympic medal chart with 25 gold medals. It has dominated the sport since 1912 and is closely followed by the public. It has triumphed in all disciplines, but it takes two to win gold: a top-trained rider and a well-bred horse.

Ian Millar

Canadian show jumper Millar holds the record for the most Olympic appearances, having competed in 10 games (1972–1976, 1984–2012). Nicknamed "Captain Canada," he won silver in the 2008 games riding In Style, a brown Hosteiner gelding.

All-Stars

Isabell Werth

 1991–   Germany

Werth has more Olympic medals (six gold and four silver) than any other dressage equestrian. She amassed 41 medals from World Cup championships, many of them on Gigolo FRH, her chestnut Hanoverian gelding.

Reiner Klimke

 1959–1999   Germany

With the second highest tally of Olympic equestrian medals (six gold and two bronze), Klimke competed in his first Olympic dressage in 1964 and was planning his sixth Olympics (Sydney 2000) when he died, aged 63.

Emma Booth

2011–   Australia

Booth started riding at age 11, but in 2013 an accident left her a paraplegic. Within seven months she was back on a horse, a year later competing in para dressage and, in 2016, representing Australia at the Paralympics.

World Equestrian Games

FEI

The World Equestrian Games, organized by Fèdèration Equestre Internationale (FEI), is held every four years – two years after a Summer Olympics – and hosted by different countries. Competitions include dressage, endurance riding, eventing, show jumping, vaulting, combined driving, reining and para equestrian events. Germany (including West Germany/FRG medals) has topped the gold medal table for many years.

Most successful riders*

		●	●	●	○
Eventing					
Blyth Tait	NZL	4	0	0	4
Show jumping					
Eric Navet	FRA	3	3	0	6
Dressage					
Isabell Werth	GER	7	0	2	9

Winners of five-plus gold, by country*

	●	●	●	○
Germany	36	26	25	87
GBR	19	20	10	49
Netherlands	17	13	16	46
USA	13	14	15	42
France	9	15	7	31
Belgium	5	6	2	13
New Zealand	5	1	2	8

* Includes all individual and team events after 1990.

Factfile

Boyd Exell

Australian Exell dominates the thrilling four-in-hand (two pairs of horses) carriage driving event. With his superlative skills, he has won seven World Cup driving titles and been World Champion four times.

Joanne Eccles

This British rider has won three gold medals at World Equestrian Games and World Championships, in vaulting. Vaulting combines gymnastics and dance on horseback. Her one-handed handstand on a cantering horse was a world first!

ARCHERY

Once a skill used for hunting and combat, archery became a competitive sport around 180 years ago. This encouraged engineers to design improved equipment, resulting in compound and recurve bows that can propel an arrow at over 120 mph! As a sport, it requires totally steady nerves, a perfect stance, accuracy, focus, an understanding of physics and flight, and endless practice. The two main events are indoor and outdoor target archery (targets at set distances) and field archery (targets in a wooded setting) for individuals and teams. Hitting the bull's-eye scores 10 points, and archers must shoot a set number of arrows in a specified time.

> "What makes an archer a champion is their psychological quality, and the confidence they give out… to control the match."
>
> Zhang JuanJuan, two-time Olympic competitor (2004, 2008)

All-Stars

Kim Soo-nyung

🕐 1988–2003   🏳 South Korea

Kim won four golds in the Olympics and World Championships. Nicknamed "The Viper" for her accuracy, her South Korean team steamrollered its way through events. She was named female archer of the 20th century.

Darrell Pace

🕐 1972–2006   🏳 USA

Winner of double Olympic and World Championship golds, this American set records from the start. Named male archer of the 20th century, Pace would train late into the night using the headlights on his truck to light the range and the target.

Hubert van Innis

🕐 c.1900–1933   🏳 Belgium

In the 1900 and 1920 Olympic Games, van Innis won nine medals. Archery rules have changed since, but this Belgian is still on the top-50 medalist list. This steady-nerved veteran last won archery gold at 67 years of age!

World Archery Championships

 WA

This event has been running since 1931. At the championships and at World Games, recurve, compound and bare bows are used. Alongside indoor and outdoor target archery, World Games have field archery events, where targets are set over different terrains, distances and in light and shade. There are also championships in para archery. In this, competitors may shoot from a sitting or standing position.

Most individual recurve* gold medals

👤	🏳	⚫	⚫	⚪	
Men					
Hans Deutgen	SWE	4	1	0	5
Women					
Janina Kurkowska-Spychajowa	POL	5	1	3	9

Most individual compound* gold medals

👤	🏳	⚫	⚫	⚪	
Men					
Stephan Hansen	DEN	1	1	0	2
Morgan Lundin	SWE	1	1	0	2
Reo Wilde	USA	1	0	1	2
Clint Freeman	AUS	1	0	1	2
Women					
Albina Loginova	RUS	2	1	0	3

* **Recurve bow**: the traditional set up of frame with outwardly curved ends and string. The differently shaped compound bow has wheels and pulleys that increase accuracy.

Factfile

Janina Kurkowska-Spychajowa

Her record of five titles in outdoor archery World Championships is unbeaten to date. She targeted and hit her first gold in 1933, and 22 years later, in 1955, won her last bronze. Kurkowska-Spychajowa's total team and individual medal haul was 19.

Mel Clarke

This GBR wheelchair para archer was in an able-bodied archery competition when she contracted Lyme disease, which affected her sight. She modified her shooting technique and won gold and silver medals in individual and team World Championships.

Focus on the Olympics

First competed in the 1900 Olympics, and then in 1908 and 1920, events included target archery and "moving bird," which involved knocking a bird-shaped target off of a beam. After a 52-year break, archery reappeared at the 1972 games. Individuals and teams use recurve bows and shoot 72 arrows at a target 70 meters away. The highest-ever Olympic score for 72 arrows was 700 out of a perfect 720.

Multiple gold medalists*

👤	🏳	⚫	⚫	⚪	
Men					
Darrell Pace	USA	2	1	0	3
Jang Yong-ho	KOR	2	1	0	3
Marco Galiazzo	ITA	2	1	0	3
Park Kyung-mo	KOR	2	1	0	3
Im Dong-hyun	KOR	2	0	1	3
Justin Huish	USA	2	0	0	2
Women					
Kim Soo-nyung	KOR	4	1	1	6
Park Sung-hyun	KOR	3	1	0	4
Ki Bo-bae	KOR	3	0	1	4
Yun Mi-jin	KOR	3	0	0	3
Lee Sung-jin	KOR	2	1	0	3
Cho Youn-jeong	KOR	2	0	0	2
Chang Hye-jin	KOR	2	0	0	2
Kim Kyung-wook	KOR	2	0	0	2

* Medals won in individual and team events since 1972.

Factfile

South Korea

Since first competing in archery at the Olympics in 1972, the South Korean team have won 23 of the possible 34 gold medals. Two of the country's most-medaled athletes are archers, and South Korea holds 13 of the 15 Olympic records.

Matt Stutzman

Known as the "Armless Archer," American Stutzman shoots seated, the bow held between his toes and the arrow supported on his chest. He set a World Record hitting a target at 283.5 meters, and won Paralympic silver in 2012.

SHOOTING

This sport is a test of nerves, concentration and accuracy. Sport shooting clubs have been around for 500 years, but the first major event was held at the 1896 Olympics. There are three main events for individuals and teams: pistol, rifle and shotgun. Pistol and rifle competitions are held on shooting ranges with the bull's-eye targets at 10, 25 or 50 meters. Competitors shoot from standing, kneeling and prone positions. In trap and skeet shotgun events, the targets are clay disks that are propelled at various heights, angles and speeds from machines. Shooters use relaxation techniques to lower their heart rate, and try to fire shots between heartbeats.

> "I was thinking I already had the gold medal. The bullet wasn't like the rest of them. It sounded different."
> Abdulla Sultan Alaryani, on losing gold in the 2016 Paralympic shooting final

World Shooting Championships ▼ [ISSF]

These shooting championships are held every four years. The first event was held in 1897. Over the years, the number of individual and team events has increased from nine to approximately 50. Since World War II, the championships have been won by only five countries: Sweden, Finland, USA, the Soviet Union and China. It's an impressive record, considering that almost 100 countries compete.

All-time multiple medalists*

👤	🚩	●	●	●	○
Konrad Staeheli	SUI	41	17	11	69
Karl Zimmermann	SUI	30	17	20	67
Lones Wigger	USA	22	22	7	51
Kullervo Leskinen	FIN	15	19	11	45
Josias Hartmann	SUI	15	12	11	38
Wilhelm Schnyder	SUI	14	2	3	19
John Robert Foster	USA	13	15	2	30
Paul Van Asbroeck	BEL	13	9	13	35
Emil Kellenberger	SUI	13	7	0	20
Gennadi Lushikov	URS	13	6	2	21
Lubos Racansky	CZE	13	5	1	19
Louis Richardet	SUI	13	4	5	22
Moysey Itkis	URS	13	1	5	19
Walter Lienhard	SUI	12	11	3	26
Otto Horber	SUI	12	9	12	33

* Includes all individual and team events and all current and discontinued events.

Factfile

 Konrad Staeheli

This Swiss sport shooter dominated military rifle, free rifle and army pistol events between 1898–1914 in World Championships (69 medals) and Olympics (4 medals). Staeheli was also the first to score more than 1,000 points in free rifle.

 Soviet Union

Until the dissolution of the Soviet Union in 1991, its individual and team shooters topped the World Championship medal table with 258 gold, 162 silver and 106 bronze. It still leads the current medal leaders, USA, by 60 golds.

All-Stars

Kimberly Rhode
 1992–   🚩 USA

Rhode is the most successful female shooter, holding six Olympic medals for double trap and skeet. At the 2012 games, this American shot 99 out of 100 clays in the skeet, and shot a perfect round in a World Cup competition final in 2007!

Guo Wenjun
 2008–   🚩 China

This Chinese sport shooter shares the team World Record for top score (1,161) in the 10-meter air pistol. She has won two Olympic golds and was the first woman to have successfully defended her Olympic title.

Carl Osburn
 1912–1924   🚩 USA

This American naval commander holds the record for the greatest number of Olympic shooting medals – 11 in total. Osburn's team and individual events were free rifle, small-bore rifle, running target and military rifle.

Focus on the Olympics 🔥

Shooting has been a feature of every Olympics since 1896 save two. Before clays were introduced, competitors shot at live pigeons. Women started competing in 1984, and the para shooting program started in 1976. Currently, the US team tops the Olympic medal table with 54 golds. China, in second place, has 22 golds. South Korea and Sweden tie for most golds (23) in para shooting.

Multiple gold medalists, current program*

👤	🚩	●	●	●	○
Men					
Ralf Schumann	GER	3	2	0	5
Jin Jong-oh	KOR	3	1	0	4
Wang Yifu	CHN	2	2	0	4
Károly Takács	HUN	2	0	0	2
Niccolò Campriani	ITA	2	0	0	2
Malcolm Cooper	GBR	2	0	0	2
Vincent Hancock	USA	2	0	0	2
Michael Diamond	AUS	2	0	0	2
Women					
Maria Grozdeva	HUN	2	0	0	2

* **Current program**: this includes using air pistol, air rifle, rapid fire pistol, rifle three positions, skeet and trap.

Most Olympic gold medals of all time

👤	🚩	●	●	●	○
Carl Osburn	USA	5	4	2	11
Kimberly Rhode	USA	3	1	2	6

Factfile

 Baron Pierre de Coubertin

Before founding the modern Olympic movement and becoming president of the International Olympic Committee (IOC), de Coubertin was the French pistol champion. He made sure a shooting event was held in the 1896 Olympics.

 Jonas Jacobsson

This Swedish sport shooter has competed in every Paralympics since 1980. His medal haul of 30, including 17 gold, puts Jacobsson in fourth place on the medal chart. In addition, he has 17 World and 22 European titles. He retired in 2016.

CYCLING

Cycle racing happens on roads, purpose-built tracks and off road. There are cycle races for individuals and teams. Road events include time trials against the clock and staged races, like the Tour de France. Road bikes have drop handles, narrow tires and single or fixed multiple gears. Track race events, mostly held indoors in velodromes, include sprints, endurance, pursuit, scratch and more. Track circuits are 250 meters and have two banked (to 45°) turns and two straights. Aerodynamic, carbon-fiber track bikes have a single gear and no brakes. There are track and cross-country sprints for BMX and mountain bikes, and endurance and downhill for mountain bikes.

> "Training is like fighting with a gorilla. You don't stop when you're tired. You stop when the gorilla is tired."
>
> Greg Henderson, former track and road pro cyclist

All-Stars

Marianne Vos
2006–   Netherlands

Often compared to Eddy Merckx, this Dutch road, cyclo-cross, mountain bike and track cyclist has medaled in World Championships and Olympics and won grand tours, stage races, road world cups and one-day races. A legend!

Jason Kenny
2005–   GBR

This track sprinter shares top rank with Sir Chris Hoy for most Olympic gold cycling medals. In 2012, Kenny, Hoy and Philip Hindes set a team sprint World Record of 42.6 secs. In his final lap, Kenny set an Olympic Record.

Mat Hoffman
1989–2002   USA

"The Condor" is a BMX vert ramp hero, winning his first pro contest at 17. This American did the first 180° backflip and, in 2002, the no-handed 900 (only successfully completed once since). Hoffman has developed scores of tricks.

Record Breakers

World Records, men's track cycling

⏱	🏃	🚩
	Flying 200-m time trial	
9.347	François Pervis	FRA
	250-m time trial	
16.984	Rene Enders	GER
	Flying 500-m time trial	
24.758	Chris Hoy	GBR
	1-km time trial	
56.303	François Pervis	FRA
	1-km time trial*	
59.340	Matthew Glaetzer	AUS
	1-km madison time trial	
54.446	Ed Clancy, George Atkins	GBR
	Team sprint (3 laps)	
41.871	Rene Enders, Robert Förstemann, Joachim Eilers	GER
	4,000-m individual pursuit	
4:10.534	Jack Bobridge	AUS
	4,000-m team pursuit	
3:49.804	Leigh Howard, Sam Welsford, Kelland O'Brien, Alex Porter	AUS

World Records, women's track cycling

⏱	🏃	🚩
	Flying 200-m time trial	
10.384	Kristina Vogel	GER
	250-m time trial	
18.282	Gong Jinjie	CHN
	Flying 500-m time trial	
28.970	Kristina Vogel	GER
	500-m time trial	
32.268	Jessica Salazar	MEX
	500-m time trial*	
32.959	Anastasiia Voinova	RUS
	Team sprint (2 laps)	
31.928	Gong Jinjie, Zhong Tianshi	CHN
	Flying 1-km time trial	
1:05.232	Erika Salumäe	URS
	3,000-m individual pursuit	
3:20.060	Chloe Dygert	USA
	3,000-m individual pursuit*	
3:22.920	Chloe Dygert	USA
	3,000-m team pursuit	
3:14.051	Dani King, Laura Trott, Joanna Rowsell	GBR
	4,000-m team pursuit	
4:10.236	Katie Archibald, Laura Trott, Elinor Barker, Joanna Rowsell	GBR

* These men's, women's and team records were set at sea level. The others were set at altitude.

One-hour records*, track

👤	🚩	▶
Men		
Bradley Wiggins	GBR	54.526 km
Chris Boardman*	GBR	56.375 km
Women		
Evelyn Stevens	USA	47.980 km
Jeannie Longo-Ciprelli*	FRA	48.159 km

* **One-hour records:** the longest distance traveled in an hour on a track by a lone cyclist. The entries marked with * were records set 1997–2014 using equipment similar to Eddy Merckx's 1972 record bike. The other records were set post-2014 on current endurance track bikes.

24-hour track record, men's

👤	🚩	▶
⚑ Indoor		
Marko Baloh	SLO	903 km
⚑ Outdoor		
Marko Baloh	SLO	890 km

24-hour track record, women's

👤	🚩	▶
⚑ Indoor		
Anna Mei	ITA	739 km
⚑ Outdoor		
Seana Hogan	USA	716 km

24-hour track record, road

👤	🚩	▶
Men		
Christoph Strasser	AUT	896 km
Women		
Maria Parker	USA	755.101 km

1,000-miles record, road

👤	🚩	⏱
Men		
Gethin Butler	GBR	55 hrs 59 mins
Women		
Lynne Taylor	GBR	64 hrs 38 mins

Race Across America*

👤	🚩	📈
Men's solo		
Christoph Strasser	AUT	⏱ 7 days, 15 hrs, 56 mins
		▶ 4,860 km
Women's solo		
Seana Hogan	USA	⏱ 9 days, 4 hrs, 2 mins
		▶ 4,686 km

* **Race Across America (RAAM):** an ultramarathon bicycle race across the US that started in 1982. It is the world's longest continuous cycling trial.

Track Cycling World Championships

UCI

These annual championships were first held in 1893. Both amateurs and professionals can enter on behalf of their country. Events include time trials, keirin, individual and team sprints and pursuits, points race, scratch races, omniums and madisons. Race distances for women's events are usually shorter. France currently tops the medal table with 141 gold, followed by the United Kingdom, the Netherlands and Australia.

Men's event* specialists, by gold

Event	Cyclist	Country	●	●	○	
Sprint	Koichi Nakano	JPN	10	0	0	10
1-km time trial	Arnaud Tournant	FRA	4	2	1	7
Individual pursuit	Hugh Porter	GBR	4	2	2	8
Keirin	Chris Hoy	GBR	4	1	0	5
Scratch	Franco Marvulli	SUI	2	0	0	2
	Alex Rasmussen	DEN	2	0	0	2
Points race	Urs Freuler	SUI	8	0	0	8
Madison	Morgan Kneisky	FRA	3	2	0	5
	Joan Llaneras	ESP	3	2	0	5
Omnium	Fernando Gaviria	COL	2	0	0	2
Team pursuit	Edward Clancy	GBR	5	4	1	10
Team sprint	Arnaud Tournant	FRA	9	1	0	10

Women's event* specialists, by gold

Event	Cyclist	Country	●	●	○	
Sprint	Galina Yermolayeva	URS	6	5	3	14
500-m time trial	Natalya Tsylinskaya	BEL	5	0	0	5
	Félicia Ballanger	FRA	5	0	0	5
Individual pursuit	Rebecca Twigg	USA	6	1	0	7
	Tamara Garkuchina	URS	6	1	0	7
Keirin	Anna Meares	AUS	3	3	1	7
Scratch	Yumari González	CUB	3	2	0	5
Points race	Ingrid Haringa	NED	4	0	0	4
Madison	Emily Nelson	GBR	1	1	0	2
Omnium	Laura Trott	GBR	2	3	0	5
Team pursuit	Joanna Rowsell	GBR	4	2	1	7
Team sprint	Miriam Welte	GER	4	0	2	6
	Kristina Vogel	GER	4	0	2	6

* **Sprint:** 250–1,000-m race for two cyclists or teams; **Keirin:** speed-controlled start followed by a sprint; **Pursuit:** two cyclists or teams, starting on opposite sides of the track, chase each over 3–4 km; **Scratch:** cyclists leave the race when lapped by the main group of cyclists; **Points:** 25–40-km race with points for winners of sprint sections; **Madison:** 30–50-km relay race; **Omnium:** six events over two days.

Factfile

 Arnaud Tournant

This French track cyclist has won multiple Olympic and World Championship medals. He set his first 1-km record (1:00.148) in 2000. A year later he broke it, becoming the first to go under a minute (58.875).

Rainbow jersey

The winners of UCI road, track, BMX and cyclo-cross championships get to wear the rainbow jersey (a white top with five colored bands across the chest). The jersey makes it easier to spot the title holder in a race, but makes it harder for him or her to launch an attack.

Road World Championships

UCI

First held in 1921 for amateur road cyclists, professional (elite) races started in 1927. Held in different locations each year, some years the course may favor sprinters who prefer a flat course, or suit climbing specialists looking for hills. Every event also includes individual time trials. The winner of this championship, the Tour de France and the Giro d'Italia is awarded the Triple Crown of Cycling.

Three-time road race* winners

	Country	●	●	○	
Men					
Alfredo Binda	ITA	3	0	1	4
Rik Van Steenbergen	BEL	3	0	1	4
Óscar Freire	ESP	3	0	1	4
Eddy Merckx	BEL	3	0	0	3
Peter Sagan	SVK	3	0	0	3
Women					
Jeannie Longo	FRA	5	2	1	8
Yvonne Reynders	BEL	4	2	1	7
Marianne Vos	NED	3	5	0	8

* **Road race:** held on paved roads, races run for around eight days and are entered by national teams. There is a mass start (all cyclists set off at the same time) and day-race distances range from 16–280 km depending on gender and age. There are separate events for juniors and under-23s.

Multiple time trial* winners

	Country	●	●	○	
Men					
Tony Martin	GER	4	1	2	7
Fabian Cancellara	SUI	4	0	3	7
Michael Rogers	AUS	3	0	0	3
Jan Ullrich	GER	2	0	1	3
Women					
Jeannie Longo	FRA	4	1	1	6
Judith Arndt	GER	2	3	2	7
Kristin Armstrong	USA	2	1	1	4
Karin Thürig	SUI	2	1	1	4
Leontien van Moorsel	NED	2	0	0	2
Amber Neben	USA	2	0	0	2

* **Time trial:** held on paved roads, the cyclists set off one by one or in national teams to complete the mixed course in the fastest possible time. Course distances vary according to gender and age.

Factfile

 Jeannie Longo

Longo's track and road cycling career spanned 37 years and included seven Olympic Games and 13 Road World Championships. The French cyclist collected multiple medals and was World Champion 13 times. Her reputation was clouded by suspicions of doping.

 Alejandro Valverde

Valverde started racing and winning when he was nine. "The Unbeatable" is today known as the "Green Bullet." This Spanish road cyclist – a climber, sprinter and time trialist – has six podium finishes, but has never managed to become World Champion.

Eddy Merckx

This Belgian cycling legend won the World Championships three times in 1967, 1971 and 1974.

Kristin Armstrong

Armstrong won the 2016 Olympic time trial – the oldest female cyclist to win gold.

Jan Ullrich

Between 2000–2004, Ullrich could not catch Lance Armstrong. But like Armstrong, he has admitted to doping.

Mountain Bike World Championships

With the rise in popularity of this sport, the first World Championships were held in 1990, with downhill and cross-country events. Today, there are 12 events, including four-cross (four racers, downhill on a prepared track) and team relay. The championships are held annually and teams represent their country.

Cross-country* multiple winners

Men		
Nino Schurter	SUI	6
Julien Absalon	FRA	5
Henrik Djernis	DEN	3
Roland Green	CAN	2
Women		
Gunn-Rita Dahle	NOR	4
Alison Sydor	CAN	3
Margarita Fullana	ESP	3
Irina Kalentieva	RUS	2
Paola Pezzo	ITA	2
Julie Bresset	FRA	2
Catharine Pendrel	CAN	2

Downhill* multiple winners

Men		
Nicolas Vouilloz	FRA	7
Greg Minnaar	RSA	3
Sam Hill	AUS	3
Gee Atherton	GBR	2
Fabien Barel	FRA	2
Loïc Bruni	FRA	2
Danny Hart	GBR	2
Women		
Anne-Caroline Chausson	FRA	9
Rachel Atherton	GBR	4
Sabrina Jonnier	FRA	2
Emmeline Ragot	FRA	2
Giovanna Bonazzi	ITA	2

* **Cross-country**: raced on the lightest mountain bikes, riders negotiate rough forest tracks, trails and fire roads in a course set in natural terrain.

* **Downhill**: raced on heavy, sturdy bikes, riders have to complete a steep, rough course with jumps, drops and other obstacles.

Anne-Caroline Chausson
Her one Olympic gold is dwarfed by 16 World Championship gold medals.

BMX World Championships

Held annually over three days since 1996 (though the first World Championships were held in 1986), the current overall medal leader is the USA. BMX (bicycle motocross) is held on a purpose-built dirt track with flat sections, banked corners, jumps and rollers. Eight racers leave the start gate at one time to negotiate the 300–400-meter course.

Multiple elite titles

Men		
Kyle Bennett	USA	3
Dale Holmes	GBR	2
Thomas Allier	FRA	2
Maris Strombergs	LAT	2
Sam Willoughby	AUS	2
Joris Daudet	FRA	2
Women		
Gabriela Díaz	ARG	3
Shanaze Reade	GBR	3
Mariana Pajon	COL	3
Natarsha Williams	AUS	2
Willy Kanis	NED	2

In the all-time table to 2017, the US tops the medal count with 101, though France is close behind with 99. Australia sits in third with 48 points.

Factfile

 Kyle Bennett

Nicknamed "Butter" for his smooth riding, this BMX racer and dirt jumper was Elite World Champion three times, and on the first US BMX Olympic team. He died in an accident in 2012.

 Gabriela Díaz

This BMX racer won five medals at the championships between 2000 and 2006, setting a women's record. In the women's elite rankings and 16 years after her first race, Díaz sits at No. 16.

Focus on the Olympics

While men's cycling events have been on the Olympic schedule since 1896, women's events only began in 1984. There are currently six track events (keirin, madison, omnium, individual and team sprints, and team pursuit), two road races, cross country and two BMX competitions (racing and freestyle). A keirin is a 1.5-km race with a controlled speed start (three laps) followed by a sprint (three laps).

Multiple gold medalists by event, men

			●	●	●	○
Track cycling, keirin						
Chris Hoy	GBR		2	0	0	2
Track cycling, individual sprint						
Daniel Morelon	FRA		2	1	1	4
Track cycling, team sprint						
Jason Kenny	GBR		3	0	0	3
Track cycling, team pursuit						
Ed Clancy	GBR		3	0	0	3
Road cycling, time trial						
Viatcheslav Ekimov	RUS		2	0	0	2
Fabian Cancellara	SUI		2	0	0	2
Mountain bike, cross-country						
Julien Absalon	FRA		2	0	0	2
BMX racing						
Māris Štrombergs	LAT		2	0	0	2

Most successful overall gold medalists, men

			●	●	●	○
Chris Hoy	GBR		6	1	0	7
Jason Kenny	GBR		6	1	0	7

Multiple gold medalists by event*, women

			●	●	●	○
Track cycling, omnium						
Laura Trott	GBR		2	0	0	2
Track cycling, individual sprint						
Félicia Ballanger	FRA		2	0	0	2
Erika Salumäe	URS/EST		2	0	0	2
Track cycling, team pursuit						
Laura Trott	GBR		2	0	0	2
Road cycling, time trial						
Kristin Armstrong	USA		3	0	0	3
Mountain bike, cross-country						
Paola Pezzo	ITA		2	0	0	2
BMX racing						
Mariana Pajón	COL		2	0	0	2

* Women's madison to debut in the 2020 Olympics.

Most successful overall gold medalists, women

			●	●	●	○
Leontien van Moorsel	NED		4	1	1	6

Factfile

 Chris Hoy

Considered one of the most successful male Olympic track cyclists of all time (six golds and one bronze), the Scottish Hoy has also won multiple golds in World Cup and Commonwealth events. His specialties are sprints and keirin.

 Leontien van Moorsel

Van Moorsel, the "queen of road and track cycling" (1990–2004) set an hour record (43.065 km) for women that stood for 12 years. After dealing with eating disorders, van Moorsel crashed badly in the 2004 Olympic road race, but went on to win gold.

Tour de France

Possibly the grandest of the three Grand Tour races, the Tour de France consists of flat and hilly sections, mountain stages and time trials. Some 20–22 teams, with nine male riders per team, cover around 3,400 km in 21 days. The 2018 race included 21 stages. This grueling road race was started in 1903. At the end of each stage, the cyclist with the fastest cumulative time wears the coveted yellow jersey.

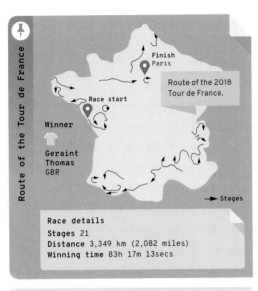

Route of the 2018 Tour de France.

Finish
Paris

Race start

Winner

Geraint Thomas GBR

→ Stages

Route of the Tour de France

Race details
Stages 21
Distance 3,349 km (2,082 miles)
Winning time 83h 17m 13secs

La Course is the women's road race, run during the Tour, which uses one or two stages of the Tour course.

General classification*

		👕	📅
Jacques Anquetil	FRA	5	1957, 1961, 1962, 1963, 1964
Eddy Merckx	BEL	5	1969, 1970, 1971, 1972, 1974
Bernard Hinault	FRA	5	1978, 1979, 1981, 1982, 1985
Miguel Induráin	ESP	5	1991, 1992, 1993, 1994, 1995

* **General classification**: in the Tour, this determines the overall and ultimate winner who will wear the yellow jersey.

Mountain classification*

		👕	📅
Richard Virenque	FRA	7	1994, 1995, 1996, 1997, 1999, 2003, 2004
Federico Bahamontes	ESP	6	1954, 1958, 1959, 1962, 1963, 1964
Lucien Van Impe	BEL	6	1971, 1972, 1975, 1977, 1981, 1983
Julio Jiménez	ESP	3	1965, 1966, 1967

* **Mountain classification**: this is won by the rider who gains the most points for reaching summits first. The winner wears a red polka-dot jersey.

Factfile

Not quite teammates!
Greg LeMond v. Bernard Hinault

In 1985, American LeMond helped his French teammate win his fifth Tour. In 1986, Hinault was supposed to return the favor, but he had other ideas and took the yellow jersey in one stage. Despite this, LeMond won the Tour, with Hinault coming in second.

Miguel Induráin

This Spanish cyclist now holds the record for the most consecutive Tour wins – five times between 1991–1995 – after Lance Armstrong's record was revoked. Induráin is among the few who have twice won the Tour de France and Giro d'Italia double in one season.

A Moment in Time

Times were different then

📅 July 2–24, 1904

📍 Various stages, France

🏁 Le Tour de France

This Tour was very eventful. Cyclist Hippolyte Aucouturier was towed around one stage of the race, and Maurice Garin (who smoked while he rode) took a train for part of a stage. Garin also put itching powder down rivals' shorts and arranged for his supporters to hit rivals with sticks as they rode by.

Controversy

Contentious silver

👤 Mark Cavendish

📅 August 15, 2016

📍 Points race, men's omnium final

🏁 Summer Olympics, Rio

Cavendish waited eight years for an Olympic medal, but perhaps it arrived a little tarnished. He was in second overall before the last event, when he crashed into Sanghoon Park and race leader, Elia Viviani. Viviani got back on his bike for gold and Cavendish held on to second place for the silver.

Para Cycling

There are 18 velodrome and 33 road event medals up for grabs at the Paralympics. Cyclists with visual or limb impairments, or cerebral palsy, compete on bicycles, tricycles, handcycles and tandems (the visually impaired cyclist sits at the rear). There are road races, time trials, relays, sprints, pursuit and scratch races. Elite para cyclists also compete in World Championships and World Cups.

Paralympic medal leaders, by country

🏁	●	●	●	○
GBR	41	19	13	73
Australia	37	31	29	97
USA	23	39	29	91
Germany	20	24	17	61
Italy	16	10	13	39
France	13	7	14	34
Spain	11	15	16	42
Netherlands	10	13	12	35
China	10	11	14	35
Canada	9	11	13	33

Cyclist with most Paralympic gold

👤	🏁	●	●	●	○
Men					
Jiri Jezek	CZE	6	4	1	11
Darren Kenny	GBR	6	3	1	10
Christopher Scott	AUS	6	2	2	10
Women					
Sarah Storey	GBR	9	0	0	9

Superstars ★

Lindy Hou

This Australian para cyclist and triathlete was declared legally blind in 1996. Riding tandem bikes with her sighted pilots, Janelle Lindsay and Toireasa Gallagher, she competed in sprint, pursuit and road races. Over two Paralympics, she and her pilots won six medals.

🔄 2004–2014   🏁 Australia

Para Athletes

VOLLEYBALL

Starting as an indoor game in 1895, volleyball has two teams of six players, with the aim to score points by grounding the ball on the opponent's side of the net. The ball is not thrown, but propelled by hitting it with the hands or arms. Beach volleyball, recognized in 1987, is played by two teams of two players on a sand court. Indoor first appeared in the Olympics in 1964, and beach volleyball in 1996. The Paralympic format, called sitting volleyball, is played indoors on a slightly smaller court, and players' pelvises must be in contact with the floor at all times. All volleyball games are fast, noisy (players constantly communicate) and feverishly competitive!

> **"The volleyball player is not a soloist, but a member of an orchestra. When that player begins to think, 'I'm special,' the player is finished."**
> Bernardo Rezende, coach and former player

All-Stars

Karch Kiraly

1977–2007   USA

A master at indoor and beach volleyball, Kiraly won 148 events including three US national titles, three Olympic golds, two World Championships, and was a four-time All-American. He was named Best Player in the World twice.

Regla Torres

1983–2005   Cuba

This indoor volleyball middle blocker and hitter was the youngest volleyball Olympic gold-medal winner at the age of 17. Torres has added two more Olympic golds to her tally and been named Best Volleyball Player of the 20th Century.

Kaleo Kanahele

2010–   USA

Born with a club left foot, Kanahele took up sitting volleyball at age nine. Since playing competitively, she has won five gold and two silver medals at the Parapan American Championships, Masters, Paralympics and World Championships.

▼ Volleyball World Championship   FIVB

Federation Internationale de Volleyball (FIVB) World Championships predate Olympic appearances by almost 20 years. Though both the indoor and beach games were already popular, the FIVB competitions made volleyball one of the top five international sports in the world. At the 2018 Winter Games, an exhibition snow volleyball match was played. (Beach volleyball bathing suits were swapped for thermals.)

Men's medals summary, by gold

🏳	●	●	●	○
Russia	6	3	3	12
Brazil	3	2	0	5
Italy	3	1	0	4
Czech Republic	2	4	0	6
Poland*	2	1	0	3
Germany	1	0	1	2
USA	1	0	1	2

Women's medals summary, by gold

🏳	●	●	●	○
Russia	7	2	4	13
Japan	3	3	1	7
Cuba	3	1	0	4
China	2	3	0	5
USA*	1	2	2	5
Italy	1	0	0	1

*The 2014 men's championships were won by Poland; the women's by the USA.

Factfile

Russia

The Russian men's volleyball teams started winning in 1949 in European and World Championships and Cups, and at the Olympics. Much of the team's success is due to Nikolay Karpol, one of the longest-serving coaches in world volleyball.

Patience plays off
Brazil v. Poland

In the men's indoor World Championship final of 2014, three-time defending champs Brazil were brought down by the Polish upstarts 19–25. This broke Poland's 40-year gold-medal drought, and they did it in front of a home crowd.

Focus on the Olympics

Beach Volleyball

When two epic American men's teams faced each other in the finals at the 1996 Olympics, it revolutionized the game's tactics and made its acceptance as an official event inevitable. Currently 24 teams take part, and matches have been played against backgrounds as diverse as Bondi Beach, Australia, and Horse Guards Parade, UK.

Men's team medals summary, by gold

🏳	●	●	●	○
USA	3	1	0	4
Brazil	2	3	1	6
Germany	1	0	1	2
Italy	0	1	0	1
Spain	0	1	0	1
Canada	0	0	1	1
Latvia	0	0	1	1
Netherlands	0	0	1	1
Switzerland	0	0	1	1

Women's team medals summary, by gold

🏳	●	●	●	○
USA	3	1	2	6
Brazil	1	4	2	7
Australia	1	0	1	2
Germany	1	0	0	1
China	0	1	1	2

Factfile

Team USA

In every Olympic Games beach volleyball finals except 2016, Team USA (both men and women) has medaled. Team members Phil Dalhausser and Kerri Walsh-Jennings are beach volleyball legends and multiple winners of all-time awards.

Turning bronze to gold
Australia v. Brazil

After winning bronze in the 1996 games, the Australian women's team of Natalie Cook and Kerri Pottharst trailed in both the first and second games against Brazil in 2000, but twice dug in to win 12–11 and 12–10 to snatch Olympic gold.

OLYMPIC WEIGHTLIFTING

In this sport, athletes attempt to lift a barbell weighted with plates, testing explosive strength. There are two types of lift. In the snatch, the athlete raises the barbell from the ground to overhead, arms straight, in one continuous move. For the clean and jerk, the barbell is raised to shoulder level and then above the head. Each athlete performs each lift three times. If there are no successful lifts, the athlete does not "total." In Paralympics, athletes with lower limb or hip impairments test their upper body strength in powerlifting. Both sports are divided into 8–10 body mass categories for men and women. Weightlifting has been an Olympic event since 1896.

> "You can be an incredible athlete who is as strong as an ox, but if you are not mentally strong, you're going to have a tough time..."
>
> Morghan King, 2016 Olympic weightlifter

All-Stars

Pyross Dimas

🕒 1989–2004   🏳 Greece

Dimas is regarded as the greatest weightlifter of all time with three Olympic golds and three World Champion titles. His career best in the 85-kg category was 180.5-kg snatch and 215-kg clean and jerk.

LeeAnn Hewitt

🕒 2015–   🏳 USA

The youngest person ever to compete in powerlifting and weightlifting at a national level, Hewitt has already broken six World Records. And all this while studying, managing her diabetes and training for future gold.

Siamand Rahman

🕒 2008–   🏳 Iran

"The strongest man in Paralympic history" has set records and then repeatedly broken those records. At Rio 2016, this powerlifter cleared 305 kg on his third lift, and in a fourth record-attempt lift Rahman hoisted 310 kg!

Record Breakers

In weightlifting, record lifts are recorded for snatch, clean and jerk, and for combined snatch/clean and jerk lifts.

Current men's World Records

56 kg			
Snatch	Wu Jingbiao	CHN	139 kg
Clean & jerk	Om Yun-chol	PRK	171 kg
Total	Long Qingquan	CHN	307 kg
62 kg			
Snatch	Kim Un-guk	PRK	154 kg
Clean & jerk	Chen Lijun	CHN	183 kg
Total	Chen Lijun	CHN	333 kg
69 kg			
Snatch	Liao Hui	CHN	166 kg
Clean & jerk	Liao Hui	CHN	198 kg
Total	Liao Hui	CHN	359 kg
77 kg			
Snatch	Lü Xiaojun	CHN	177 kg
Clean & jerk	Nijat Rahimov	KAZ	214 kg
Total	Lü Xiaojun	CHN	380 kg
85 kg			
Snatch	Andrei Rybakou	BEL	187 kg
Clean & jerk	Kianoush Rostami	IRI	220 kg
Total	Kianoush Rostami	IRI	396 kg
94 kg			
Snatch	Akakios Kakiasvilis	GRC	188 kg
Clean & jerk	Sohrab Moradi	IRI	233 kg
Total	Sohrab Moradi	IRI	417 kg
105 kg			
Snatch	Andrei Aramnau	BEL	200 kg
Clean & jerk	Ilya Ilyin	KAZ	246 kg
Total	Ilya Ilyin	KAZ	437 kg
+105 kg			
Snatch	Lasha Talakhadze	GEO	220 kg
Clean & jerk	Hossein Rezazadeh	IRI	263 kg
Total	Lasha Talakhadze	GEO	477 kg

Current women's World Records

48 kg			
Snatch	Yang Lian	CHN	98 kg
Clean & jerk	Nurcan Taylan	TUR	121 kg
Total	Yang Lian	CHN	217 kg
53 kg			
Snatch	Li Ping	CHN	103 kg
Clean & jerk	Zulfiya Chinshanlo	KAZ	134 kg
Total	Hsu Shu-ching	TPE	233 kg
58 kg			
Snatch	Boyanka Kostova	AZE	112 kg
Clean & jerk	Kuo Hsing-chun	TPE	142 kg
Total	Boyanka Kostova	AZE	252 kg
63 kg			
Snatch	Svetlana Tsarukayeva	RUS	117 kg
Clean & jerk	Deng Wei	CHN	147 kg
Total	Deng Wei	CHN	262 kg
69 kg			
Snatch	Oksana Slivenko	RUS	123 kg
Clean & jerk	Zarema Kasayeva	RUS	157 kg
Total	Oksana Slivenko	RUS	276 kg
75 kg			
Snatch	Natalia Zabolotnaya	RUS	135 kg
Clean & jerk	Kim Un-ju	PRK	164 kg
Total	Natalia Zabolotnaya	RUS	296 kg
90 kg			
Snatch	Viktoriya Shaymardanova	UKR	130 kg
Clean & jerk	Hripsime Khurshudyan	ARM	160 kg
Total	Hripsime Khurshudyan	ARM	283 kg
+90 kg			
Snatch	Tatiana Kashirina	RUS	155 kg
Clean & jerk	Tatiana Kashirina	RUS	193 kg
Total	Tatiana Kashirina	RUS	348 kg

Clean and press World Records*

52 kg	Adam Gnatov	URS	120.5 kg
56 kg	Mohammad Nassiri	IRI	128.5 kg
60 kg	Imre Földi	HUN	137.5 kg
67.5 kg	Mladen Kuchev	BUL	157.5 kg
75 kg	Aleksandr Kolodkov	URS	166.5 kg
82.5 kg	Gennady Ivanchenko	URS	178.5 kg
90 kg	David Rigert	URS	198.0 kg
110 kg	Yury Kozin	URS	213.5 kg
+110 kg	Vasily Alekseyev	URS	236.5 kg

* Clean and press: like clean and jerk, load is raised overhead but uses different technique. Records cover 1920–1972.

Six-plus medals World Championships*

		●	●	●	○
Vasily Alekseyev	URS	8	0	0	8
Yurik Vardanyan	URS	7	1	0	8
Naim Süleymanoğlu	BUL/TUR	7	1	0	8
Josef Grafl	AUT	6	2	0	8
Tommy Kono	USA	6	1	1	8
John Davis	USA	6	1	0	7
Yoshinobu Miyake	JPN	6	0	1	7
David Rigert	URS	6	0	1	7

* The weightlifting World Championships for men started in 1891 and in 1987 for women. From 1991, a combined men's and women's event was held.

Country/city codes

These are the three-letter codes used by the IOC or FIFA for countries and cities that appear in this book. Alongside countries that have changed status (gained independence) or name, start and/or end dates are provided.

 ALG Algeria

 ARG Argentina

 ARM Armenia

 AUS Australia

 AUT Austria

 AZE Azerbaijan

BEL Belgium

 BER Bermuda

 BLR Belarus

 BOL Bolivia

BRA Brazil

BRN Bahrain

BUL Bulgaria

BUR Burkina Faso

CAN Canada

CHI Chile

CHN China PR

CIV Côte d'Ivoire

CMR Cameroon

COL Colombia

CRO Croatia 1991–

CUB Cuba

CZE Czech Republic

DEN Denmark

ECU Ecuador

EGY Egypt

ENG England

ERI Eritrea

ESP Spain

EST Estonia

ETH Ethiopia

EUA United Team of Germany 1956–1964

EUN* Unified Team 1992

FIN Finland

FRA France

FRG West Germany 1949–1990

GBR Great Britain/ United Kingdom

GDR East Germany 1949–1990

 GEO Georgia

GHA Ghana

GRE Greece

HUN Hungary

INA Indonesia

IND India

IRI Iran

IRL Republic of Ireland

ISR Israel

ITA Italy

JAM Jamaica

JER Jersey

JPN Japan

KAZ Kazakhstan

KEN Kenya

KOR South Korea

LAT Latvia

LBR Liberia

LIE Liechtenstein

LTU Lithuania

LUX Luxembourg

MAR Morocco

MAS Malaysia

MEX Mexico

MNE Montenegro 2006–

NAM Namibia

NED Netherlands

NGR Nigeria

NIR Northern Ireland

NOR Norway

NZL New Zealand

OAR Olympic Athletes from Russia 2018

PAK Pakistan

PAN Panama

PAR Paraguay

POL Poland

POR Portugal

PRK North Korea

PUR Puerto Rico

QAT Qatar

ROU Romania

RSA South Africa

RUS Russia 1991–

SCG Serbia and Montenegro 1992–2006

SCO Scotland

SEN Senegal

SLO Slovenia

SRB Serbia 2006–

SUI Switzerland

SVK Slovakia 1993–

SWE Sweden

TCH Czechoslovakia 1918–1993

THA Thailand

TPE Chinese Taipei

TUR Turkey

UAE United Arab Emirates

UKR Ukraine 1991–

URS Soviet Union 1922–1991

URU Uruguay

USA United States of America

VEN Venezuela

WAL Wales

YUG Yugoslavia 1918–1992

* EUN
Unified Team 1992 included countries of the former Soviet Union including Armenia, Azerbaijan, Belarus, Georgia, Kazakhstan, Kyrgyzstan, Moldova, Russia, Tajikistan, Turkmenistan, Ukraine and Uzbekistan.

 Sports governing bodies

These governing bodies organize major tournaments and establish the regulations of their relevant sport.

ABL Australian Baseball League

AELTC All England Lawn Tennis and Croquet Club or All England Club

AFL Arena Football League

BWF Badminton World Federation

CFL Canadian Football League

CONMEBOL South American Football Confederation

EPL English Premier League

FA Football Association

FEI Fédération Equestre Internationale

FIA Fédération Internationale de l'Automobile

FIBA Fédération Internationale de Basketball

FIFA Fédération Internationale de Football Association

FIM Fédération Internationale de Motocyclisme

FINA Fédération Internationale de Natation

FIS Fédération Internationale de Ski

FIVB Fédération Internationale de Volleyball

IAAF International Association of Athletics Federations

ICC International Cricket Council

ICF International Canoe Federation

IIHF International Ice Hockey Federation

INDYCAR Indy Racing League, LLC

IOC International Olympic Committee

IPC International Paralympic Committee

ISSF International Shooting Sport Federation

ITTF International Table Tennis Federation

ITU International Triathlon Union

KHL Kontinental Hockey League

LPGA Ladies Professional Golf Association

MLB Major League Baseball

MLS Major League Soccer

NASCAR National Association for Stock Car Auto Racing

NBA National Basketball Association

NFL National Football League

NHL National Hockey League

NPB Nippon Professional Baseball

PGA Professional Golf Association

PSA Professional Squash Association

RLIF Rugby League International Federation

UCI Union Cycliste Internationale

UEFA Union of European Football Associations

UFC Ultimate Fighting Championship

UIM Union Internationale Motonautique

ATP Association of Tennis Professionals

WA World Archery

WBC World Baseball Classic

WBSC World Baseball Softball Confederation

WNBA Women's National Basketball Association